Through the Lens of Faith

Through the Lens of Faith

Devotions on Life, the Universe, and Everything

ELIZABETH DANNA

RESOURCE *Publications* • Eugene, Oregon

THROUGH THE LENS OF FAITH
Devotions on Life, the Universe, and Everything

Copyright © 2022 Elizabeth Danna. All rights reserved. Except for brief quotations in critical publications or reviews, no part of this book may be reproduced in any manner without prior written permission from the publisher. Write: Permissions, Wipf and Stock Publishers, 199 W. 8th Ave., Suite 3, Eugene, OR 97401.

Resource Publications
An Imprint of Wipf and Stock Publishers
199 W. 8th Ave., Suite 3
Eugene, OR 97401

www.wipfandstock.com

PAPERBACK ISBN: 978-1-6667-9633-9
HARDCOVER ISBN: 978-1-6667-9632-2
EBOOK ISBN: 978-1-6667-9634-6

JUNE 1, 2022 1:56 PM

Scripture quotations marked (RSV) are taken from the Revised Standard Version of the Bible, copyright 1952, [2nd edition, 1971] by the Division of Christian Education of the National Council of Churches of Christ in the United States of America. Used by permission. All rights reserved.

Scripture Quotations marked (NRSV) are taken from the New Revised Standard Version Bible, copyright 1989, Division of Christian Education of the National Council of Churches of Christ in the United States of America. Used by permission. All rights reserved.

Scripture quotations marked (NIV) are taken from the Holy Bible, New International-al Version®, NIV®. Copyright© 1973, 1978, 1984 by Biblica, Inc™. All rights reserved worldwide.

Scripture quotations marked (TLB) are taken from The Living Bible copyright © 1971. Used by permission of Tyndale House Publishers, Carol Stream, Illinois 60188. All rights reserved.

In memory of my parents
Frank A. Danna (1932–1978)
and
Edith A. Danna (1931–2021)
who taught me to love music, the arts, and God's word.

Contents

Acknowledgements | xiii

List of Abbreviations | xv

Introduction | xvii

The Answer Is... | 1

Power for the Call | 2

Better Together | 3

Stopping the Bullet | 4

Jesus Our Brother | 5

Chosen | 6

Detecting Counterfeits | 7

Moving Cleopatra | 8

Forgiveness and Feelings | 9

Fortune and Men's Eyes | 10

The Death-Defier | 11

Great Power, Great Responsibility | 12

The Heavens Declare | 13

The Father of Lies | 14

More Lies | 15

In His Hand | 16

"What's That in Your Hand?" | 17

Jekyll and Hyde, Spirit and Flesh | 18

No TARDIS Required | 19

Lane-Departure Warning | 20

Like Father, Like Child | 21

The Little Things | 22

Letting Go of Guilt | 23

Examples for Tough Times | 24

Here, On the Way to There | 25

A Motley Crew | 26

Tricked | 27

Make a Joyful Noise | 28

Names of Jesus | 29

High-Performance | 30

Peace | 31

Our Last Battlefield? | 32

Change of Law, Change of Heart | 33

His Power, Our Weakness | 34

Running to Win | 35

A Safe Place | 36

The Star-Shepherd | 37

Sealed with the Spirit | 38

"Stick-to-it-iveness" | 39

For Such a Time as This | 40

The Theory of Everything | 41

Totality Doesn't Last Forever | 42

Unprecedented Christmas | 43

Watch Your Mouth | 44

To Know What Love Is | 45

The Whole World is Watching | 46

Bought with a Price | 47

Abiding in the Vine | 48

Ambassadors of Christ | 49

Rules and Relationship | 50

As You Sow . . . | 51

A Capital Mistake | 52

A Christmas Star | 53

Couldn't He . . . ? | 54

Cupboard Love | 55

Comforted to Comfort | 56

Danger, Anger | 57

Our Ultimate Hope | 58

Thankful in All Circumstances | 59

Every Great Decision . . . | 60

A Defeated Foe | 61

When the Pressure is On | 62

Don't Look Back | 63

Fighting Fear | 64

Flowers in the Dark | 65

The Cure for Insecurity | 66

The Master Artist | 67

American Dream? | 68

Humble Enough to Dare | 69

One-of-a-Kind | 70

Back to Real Life | 71

Leave Room for Wrath | 72

The Sacrifice | 73

"Salvation Panic" | 74

Shine Like Stars | 75

Snow in April | 76

Summing Up | 77

Soon | 78

God Our Vindicator | 79

Our Unchanging God | 80

Truth | 81

Real Beauty | 82

You Can Call Anytime | 83

Not Distracted | 84

Asking and Getting | 85

Currency of a Life | 86

Do What You're Designed For | 87

All Dressed Up | 88

Hope Without Doubt | 89

The Lion and the Dragon | 90

What Do You Smell Like? | 91

The Needs of the Many | 92

Building on Two Foundations | 93

Safety in Numbers | 94

The Weak Things | 95

Why? | 96

What We Do in Life | 97

Facing the Future | 98

Different, And Needed | 99

In Jesus' Name | 100

"As I Was With Moses . . . " | 101

The Last Adam | 102

God's Endless Mercies | 103

Bring Your A-Game | 104

Superhero | 105

"That All May Be One" | 106

A Work in Progress | 107

The Church Endures | 108

Can't Undo | 109

God of the Second Chance | 110

Leap of Faith | 111

God's Covenant Care | 112

Secret Things, Revealed Things | 113

When Mordor Laughs | 114

Seventy Times Seven | 115

Custom-Built, by Hand | 116

On Prayer | 117

We Are Family | 118

Free! | 119

A Little is Enough | 120

Bibliography | 123

Acknowledgements

I WOULD LIKE TO THANK my proofreaders, Roberta Stanton-Gray and Charmain Sebestyen, for their eagle eyes and helpful suggestions. Any mistakes that remain are my own. Thanks also to Emily Callihan, Assistant Managing Editor, and the rest of the staff at Wipf & Stock for their help in getting this book into print. Above all, to God be thanks and praise.

List of Abbreviations

Old Testament

Gen	Genesis
Exod	Exodus
Lev	Leviticus
Num	Numbers
Deut	Deuteronomy
Josh	Joshua
Judg	Judges
Ruth	Ruth
1–2 Sam	1–2 Samuel
1–2 Kgs	1–2 Kings
1–2 Chron	1–2 Chronicles
Ezra	Ezra
Neh	Neh
Esth	Esther
Job	Job
Ps/Pss	Psalm/Psalms
Prov	Proverbs
Eccl	Ecclesiastes

Song	Song of Solomon
Isa	Isaiah
Jer	Jeremiah
Lam	Lamentations
Ezek	Ezekiel
Dan	Daniel
Hos	Hosea
Joel	Joel
Amos	Amos
Obad	Obadiah
Jonah	Jonah
Mic	Micah
Nah	Nahum
Hab	Habakkuk
Zeph	Zephaniah
Hag	Haggai
Zech	Zech
Mal	Malachi

List of Abbreviations

New Testament

Matt	Matthew
Mark	Mark
Luke	Luke
John	John
Acts	Acts
Rom	Romans
1–2 Cor	1–2 Corinthians
Gal	Galatians
Eph	Ephesians
Phil	Philippians
Col	Colossians

1–2 Thess	1–2 Thessalonians
1–2 Tim	1–2 Timothy
Titus	Titus
Phlm	Philemon
Heb	Hebrews
Jas	James
1–2 Pet	1–2 Peter
1–2–3 John	1–2–3 John
Jude	Jude
Rev	Revelation

Introduction

FOR THE CHRISTIAN, there are spiritual lessons to be learned from everything around us. In the realm of science and nature, creation tells us about the Creator (Ps 19:1–4). In the realm of popular culture, spiritual questions can be raised by the things we read, watch, and listen to, even if they aren't specifically Christian. For example, *Star Trek* creator Gene Roddenberry was an atheist; but his series raises issues about which the Christian can ask, "What does the Bible say about that?" Current events can also lead us to look for a biblical perspective on what's happening around us. Even our pet friends can teach us a thing or two on the spiritual level as well. And there are certain issues that arise repeatedly in ministry. The enemy sometimes tries to convince us that we're the only one who has a particular problem; but that's one of his lies.

Each daily reading begins with a Scripture reading. Then comes the reading itself, ending with a concluding thought or prayer. I've mostly used the Revised Standard Version (RSV) and the New International Version (NIV) throughout this book; you may use any version you wish. These devotions have arisen from my looking at things through the lens of faith; my hope is that you will see what you can learn if you look at things through the lens of faith.

Today's Reading: Col 1:15–18

The Answer Is...

IN DOUGLAS ADAMS'S SCIENCE-FICTION/COMEDY *The Hitchhiker's Guide to the Galaxy*, a supercomputer is asked to find the answer to the Ultimate Question of Life, the Universe, and Everything. After seven and a half million years of calculations, the computer arrives at the answer: the answer is forty-two.*

The Bible indicates that the answer to this Ultimate Question is not forty-two or any other number, but a person: Jesus. It was through Jesus that God created the universe (John 1:3,10; Heb 1:2) and it is through Jesus that God upholds it (Col 1:17; Heb 1:3). Jesus is the exact representation of God in physical form (Heb 1:3; John 1:14). Perhaps this is why Paul wrote that "Christ [is] the power of God and the wisdom of God" (1 Cor 1:24 RSV) and that "in [him] are hidden all the treasures of wisdom and knowledge" (Col 2:3 NIV). And perhaps Jesus himself summed all this up when he said, "I am the way, and the truth, and the life" (John 14:6). This means that if we want answers to life's deeper questions, we must turn to Jesus for them. And when we do, we'll find that he himself is the ultimate answer to the Ultimate Question.

All this reminds me of a scene from the 1959 version of the movie *Ben-Hur*. Ben-Hur and his new acquaintance Balthazar (formerly one of the wise men at Bethlehem) are among a crowd gathering to hear Jesus preach. Balthazar tells Ben-Hur that he knows that Jesus is the Son of God. Ben-Hur says, "Happy Balthazar. Life has answered your questions." Balthazar answers, "Life has been answered. God has answered it."**

The answer to the Ultimate Question of Life, the Universe, and Everything isn't forty-two or any other number, but a person: Jesus.

---

* Adams, *Hitchhiker's Guide*, 112-13.
** William Wyler, dir. *Ben-Hur*.

Today's Reading: Luke 24:45–49

Power for the Call

A NUMBER OF PEOPLE HAVE told me that they feel overwhelmed by the call that God has placed on their lives. They feel insufficient for the task. If this is how you feel, I have good news for you.

God doesn't call his people to do something and then leave us high and dry and unable to do it. It has been well said that those whom God calls, he equips. When Jesus commissioned the first disciples to go and preach, he first gave them understanding of the Scriptures (verse 45). He then said, "I am going to send you what my Father has promised; but stay in the city until you have been clothed with power from on high" (verse 49 NIV; compare Acts 1:4–5). They weren't even to try to do what Jesus had called them to do until he'd given them the power to do it, through the Holy Spirit. But once he had given them the power, they could do it with confidence, knowing that he was with them.

This is also what Paul says in Phil 4:11–13. He has learned that whatever his circumstances are, he can deal with them, because God will help him (verse 13 doesn't mean that God will help us do anything we want, but that he'll help us do whatever he has called us to do). This is still true today, because God hasn't changed. When God calls us to do something, he equips us with whatever we need to do it. That doesn't mean that he makes it easy, but that he'll help us do it. So we can carry out God's call on our lives with confidence.

When God calls us to do something, he gives us the power to do it.

Today's Reading: Rom 12:4–18

Better Together

LIONS HAVE ONE CHARACTERISTIC which they don't share with other felines. I don't mean the mane which is an adult male lion's crowning glory. While all other cats live alone, lions live in groups, called prides. Thousands of years ago, lions learned that they do better if they live and work together. That way they can protect each other from enemies. And lionesses hunt as a team, because it's easier that way for them to catch food.

There's a lesson here that Christians should learn too. Like lions, we do better if we work together. It's important for every Christian to be connected to a local church. The local church is the believer's support system. We are to be there for each other, in good times and bad. We should be able to count on our fellow church members for support when they need it, and they should be able to count on us. This is what it means to rejoice with those who rejoice and weep with those who weep (Rom 12:15). God gives various gifts to his people, and does this not so that they may show off to others or benefit themselves, but so that they may use their gifts to benefit and encourage others (1 Cor 14:12). Using our gifts properly means being connected to the church.

The church is also the place where we learn about God through Spirit-led preaching and group Bible study. We learn from those who have more experience in the things of God than we do. And if we struggle with any kind of sin, it's easier to stay on track with God if we're around people who are on track. It's a kind of "herd immunity" to sin.

It's important that Christians be connected to the church.

Today's reading: Ps 51:5–12

Stopping the Bullet

THE TV SERIES NUMB3RS is about a young math genius who helps his brother, an FBI agent, solve crimes (I enjoyed this series even though, I confess, I have no mathematical ability!). Charlie, the mathematician, enjoys helping Don. But by the fifth-season episode, "Guilt Trip," Charlie wants more. He says, "I feel like I've been putting Band-Aids on bullet holes. I want to find a way to stop the bullet."* He can use his mathematical skills to anticipate what a criminal will do next, so Don and his team can arrest them. But what he wants now is to find a way to stop people from wanting to commit crimes. But neither math nor police work can do that. What he's talking about is changing people's hearts. And there's only one person who can do that.

This is what David had realized when he wrote Ps 51. When he was confronted about what he'd done, he recognized his sinfulness and his need for a change of heart. But he also knew that he couldn't change his own heart. So he asked God to renew him and give him a clean heart.

What David asked for is what God promised to do for all his people in Ezek 36:26: "I will give you a new heart and put a new spirit in you; I will remove from you your heart of stone and give you a heart of flesh." And he has kept that promise, in the new covenant brought in by the death of Jesus (Heb 10:14-16). Under the new covenant, God changes us from the inside out by the working of the Holy Spirit.

Father, only you can stop sin by changing our hearts by the power of the Holy Spirit. Create in us clean hearts.

---

* Hoarder-Payton, NUMB3RS, "Guilt Trip."

Today's Reading: Eph 4:4–7

Jesus Our Brother

THERE'S AN AMUSING MOMENT near the end of *The Lion, the Witch and the Wardrobe*, the second book in C.S. Lewis's *Chronicles of Narnia* series. Aslan the great Lion has revived several animals who were turned to stone by the evil White Witch. Among these is a mortal Lion, who greets Aslan with kittenish enthusiasm. Shortly after that, Aslan deploys his forces for the hunt for the Witch; those with a keen sense of smell are to come up front with the Lions. The mortal Lion notices Aslan's phrasing, and says, "Did you hear what he said? *Us Lions*. That means him and me. *Us Lions*. That's what I like about Aslan. No side; no stand-off-ishness."* Aslan symbolizes Jesus in the world of Narnia, and reflects the character of Jesus.

This scene immediately reminded me of Hebrews 2:11, where the writer says that Jesus is not ashamed to call us his brothers. Jesus called the Twelve his brothers in Matt 28:10; John 20:17. (We may notice that that these Gospel sayings come during post-resurrection appearances, just as this Aslan scene takes place after Aslan's death and resurrection at the Stone Table). And during his ministry, Jesus didn't stay aloof from people, but shared in their daily lives, celebrations and synagogue worship (John 2:1–11; Luke 4:16). What was true then is true today; we are Jesus' brothers and sisters. Of course, there's a significant difference—Jesus is God's Son by begetting, while we're his sons and daughters by adoption (Gal 4:5; Eph 1:5). But he still identifies with us in our daily lives, sharing in our joys and our struggles. Our Brother cares about his younger brothers and sisters.

Jesus our Brother is with us in our daily lives, our joys and sorrows.

---

* Lewis, *The Chronicles of Narnia*, 190.

Today's Reading: Isa 41:9–10

Chosen

Young Sarah came home from school crying. In Phys Ed class that day they'd played baseball. Sarah had been the last child picked for a team, again.

Maybe you've felt that kind of rejection. Maybe you were the last child picked for a team, as if you just weren't good enough. Or maybe you spent many Saturday nights at home, without a date (I didn't go to my high school graduation dance, because I would have had to go alone).

I used to see myself as Little Miss Reject. I had few friends, and certainly no boyfriends. But I've learned that God has not rejected me. And he has not rejected you either. This is the assurance that God gives us in Isa 41:9 NIV: "I took you from the ends of the earth, from its farthest corners I called you. I said, 'You are my servant;' I have chosen you and have not rejected you." (This verse has become very precious to me.) And Jesus told his disciples, "You did not choose me, but I chose you (John 15:16 RSV). God chose us in Christ even before he created the world (Eph 1:4). Not that we were better than anyone else. He chose us simply because he loves us. The idea that you're not good enough is a lie from Satan.

The pain of rejection can be replaced by the knowledge that God loves us, and has chosen us. The Creator and Ruler of all things has chosen us, he loves and values us. Since God has chosen us, does it matter if we were picked last for the team?

Thank you Father that you have chosen me and not rejected me. Help me to see myself as you see me in Jesus.

Today's Reading: Ps 119:4–7, 11–16

Detecting Counterfeits

SOME YEARS AGO I worked in a local shopping mall. One day a notice came around from the local police: someone was passing counterfeit $50.00 bills. That reminded me of something I'd heard: when FBI agents learn how to detect counterfeit money, they do it by handling legal money. When they get to know the real thing, they can recognize any kind of fake. I mentioned this to a colleague who, besides working with us, also worked in a bank. She said, "It's true. When you handle enough money, you can tell when something's wrong."

Money isn't the only thing out there that could be counterfeit. There's a lot false "Bible teaching" out there, and it's doing the church a lot of harm. Jesus called such teachers wolves in sheep's clothing (Matt 7:15, compare Acts 20:29). Just as FBI agents detect counterfeit money by studying the real thing, so we can detect false teaching by studying God's truth as found in God's word. That's why Paul reminded Timothy of the importance of rightly handling the word of truth (2 Tim 2:15). We also have the Holy Spirit to teach us and guide us into all truth, and remind us of what Jesus said (John 14:26; 16:13–14). Any teaching that isn't in line with God's written word is false and should be rejected. Bible study takes time and effort. But knowing God's truth is the only way we can avoid being deceived by falsehood. This is in part what the psalmist meant when he wrote, "I have hidden your word in my heart that I might not sin against you" (Ps 119:11 NIV). Let's study the Bible and learn to recognize false teaching.

The best way to detect false teaching is to know God's truth.

Today's Reading: Ps 123:1–2

Moving Cleopatra

I RECENTLY LEARNED A THEOLOGICAL lesson from my cat, Cleopatra. In 2020 I moved house three times in three months. The first time we moved, Cleo was terrified to be in a new environment. She spent the first week hiding under the bed. The second time, she hid under the bed for only a few hours. What made the difference? Cleo herself showed me that, when I noticed how often she was beside me, in my lap, or watching me from nearby. She had realized that as long as I was around, she was safe. Her security was in me, so she kept her eyes on me. This reminded me of Ps 123:2, "As the eyes of servants look to their master, as the eyes of a maid to the hand of her mistress, so our eyes look to the LORD our God, till he have mercy upon us" (RSV)

In what or whom is my security? What or whom am I keeping my eyes on? The last several months haven't been easy. But in 2021 I moved yet again, into what I hope will be a "forever home." Whatever happens, as long as I have the Lord with me I'll be safe wherever I am. He has promised that he is with me always (Matt. 28:20) and that he'll never leave me or forsake me (Heb. 13:5).

What applies to me applies to all God's people. Our security is in God, so let's keep our eyes on him. As long as we're in his will, we're safe. His presence is with us, even when it doesn't seem like it. We'll never go through difficult times alone.

Thank you Father for your promise to be with me wherever I go. I will keep my eyes on you.

Today's Reading: Rom 8:1–4

Forgiveness and Feelings

"God has forgiven you." "But I don't feel forgiven." This exchange has occurred countless times in ministry. Many Christians have asked God to forgive them, but they don't feel like he has forgiven them. Why do they feel like this, and what can be done about it?

Some Christians think that they've gone too far, that their sin is too great for God to forgive. But that's a lie from the enemy. Can we really sin, or do anything else, and God can't handle it? There is nothing that God will not forgive those who genuinely repent. 1 John 1:9 says, "If we confess our sins, [God] is faithful and just, and will forgive our sins and cleanse us from all unrighteousness" (RSV). And Lam 3:21-23 tells us that God's mercies never come to an end. When we ask God to forgive us, he does.

Some people don't feel forgiven because they feel that they don't deserve to be forgiven. The fact is that none of us deserves to be forgiven; no human effort can earn God's forgiveness. But God doesn't forgive us because we deserve it. He forgives us because of what Jesus did on the cross. Jesus paid for our sin at Calvary, and God doesn't ask for a double payment. So he has declared us free from condemnation (Rom 8:1–4). It's important to look past our feelings and believe God's word instead of our feelings. We can believe that we are forgiven because God has said that we are. Let's believe what God says, more than we believe our feelings, and live in the forgiveness that Jesus died for us to have.

God has forgiven us, not because we deserve it, but because of what Jesus did on the cross.

Today's Reading: John 21:21–22

Fortune and Men's Eyes

OF THE 154 SONNETS written by William Shakespeare, my favorite is Sonnet 29, "When in disgrace with fortune and men's eyes" (published 1609). The second section of this poem reads, "Wishing me like to one more rich in hope/Featured like him, like him with friends possessed/Desiring this man's art and that man's scope/With what I most enjoy contented least." Simply put, the poet wants to be like men he knows who are better-looking or have more friends or more skills than he. In other words, he's comparing himself with others, and this is leading him to be discontented.

I know how easy it is to fall into the trap of comparing oneself with others. But it does us no good. This is the mistake that Peter made in his last conversation with the risen Jesus. When he asked what would happen to John, Jesus told Peter to focus on his own relationship with Jesus, not John's. Such comparison isn't what God wants. God made you *you*, not someone else. He gave you a unique combination of characteristics and gifts which makes you uniquely suited to what God has called you to do. He loves you and values you as you are. It's a mistake to jealously want someone else's characteristics, or to look down on ourselves because we have certain characteristics and not others. Let's avoid *I wish I were as smart as she is,* or *I wish I had as many friends as he does.* This kind of thinking gets our focus onto ourselves instead of God. We honor our maker when we accept ourselves and the gifts and characteristics he's given us.

Thank you, Father, that you love me and value me as I am. Remind me not to compare myself with others.

Today's Reading: 1 Cor 15:26, 51–55

The Death-Defier

I WRITE THESE WORDS THREE months after my mother went home to be with the Lord. I have no doubt that the first to welcome her was my earthly father, escorting her into our Father's presence. Like so many believers before me, I've taken comfort in Paul's death-defying words in 1 Cor 15: "The last enemy to be destroyed is death…'Death is swallowed up in victory.' 'O death, where is thy victory? O death, where is thy sting?'" (v26, 54–55 RSV) When Jesus died and came back from the dead, he beat death at its own game. He used the devil's own weapon to defeat him, using death to destroy the devil, who has the power of death. In this way he set us free from the fear of death (Heb 2:14–15). Death had no power over him, and it has no power over us either. So we don't need to be afraid of death. The process of physical death may be painful. But it ends in the joy of being with God forever.

There is comfort here for those left behind when someone dies, too. The raising of Lazarus (John 11:1–44) was just a foretaste. One day the Death-Defier will call all the righteous dead from their graves. Then he'll catch up those of his people who happen to be alive at that time. "And so we shall [all] always be with the Lord. Therefore comfort one another with these words" (1Thess 4:17–18 RSV). In due time we'll be reunited with those we've lost. This is how death will be swallowed up in victory, when death's captives are snatched out of death's grip, and death itself dies.

Jesus the Death-Defier beat death at its own game when he died and rose from the dead

Today's Reading: Phil 1:27–30

Great Power, Great Responsibility

NEAR THE BEGINNING OF the movie *Spider-Man*, Ben Parker tells his teenage nephew Peter, "With great power comes great responsibility."* He's talking about the capabilities, and responsibilities, that come with adulthood. He doesn't know that Peter has just acquired some very unusual powers.

Philippi was a designated Roman colony, and its citizens were proud of that special status. They were proud to be Roman citizens, and they knew the rights and responsibilities that came with Roman citizenship. In Phil 1:27–30, Paul talks about the responsibilities that come with being a Christian.** The Greek word translated "your manner of life" (RSV) or "conduct yourselves" (NIV) is *politeuesthe*, which means, "live as a citizen of a particular state." They may have been citizens of Philippi, but they were also citizens of heaven (Phil 3:20), and should live accordingly. But what does it mean to live like a citizen of heaven? It means to stand together in unity, working for the gospel together (verse 27) and not to be intimidated by opponents (verse 28). This unity is a mark of their salvation (verse 28, compare John 13:35) and a warning to their opponents of coming destruction. There has been a lot of disunity in the church in recent years; it sometimes seems like we're more interested in competing with each other than in spreading the gospel to the unsaved. This hardly commends the gospel to the unsaved; it only gives ammunition to our critics. If we live rightly, we won't have to be intimidated by the critics, because they'll have nothing to criticise us for (compare Titus 2:8; 1 Pet 3:16). Let's work together for the gospel like citizens of heaven should.

Father, help us to live like citizens of heaven. In Jesus' name, amen.

---

* Raimi, dir. *Spider-Man*.
** Boice, *Philippians*, 103.

Today's Reading: Ps 19

The Heavens Declare

I ENJOY LOOKING AT THE stars, although I don't often get to places where there isn't much ambient light. And I'm amazed by photographs of deep space from NASA's telescopes. For me, almost nowhere else is God's glory more clearly displayed than in the night sky. Creation itself displays the Creator's glory.

Apparently King David thought so too, because this is where he starts in Ps 19. He says that night after night the stars proclaim God's glory to the world, without a word spoken (verses 1–4). David then mentions the sun, comparing it to a bridegroom looking resplendent in his wedding finery, or an athlete joyfully running a good race (verses 5–6). David then moves from God's glory in creation to God's glory displayed in the law. God's law, says David, is good and right because it tells us how to live a good life and what sins to avoid (verses 7–11).

We can see God's glory displayed in a way that David couldn't have seen–in his greater Descendant, Jesus. John wrote, "We have seen his glory, the glory of the one and only Son, who came from the Father, full of grace and truth" (John 1:14 NIV). And Heb 1:3 says of Jesus, "He reflects the glory of God and bears the very stamp of his nature" (RSV). God's glory is displayed most clearly in Jesus the Son, who is God made flesh, God in human form.

God wants all humanity to know that he exists and that he loves us. So he shows himself to us. He did this first in creation, then in the Jewish law, and finally in Jesus.

God's glory is displayed in creation and in the law, but most clearly in Jesus.

Today's Reading: John 8:44

The Father of Lies

IN G.K. CHESTERTON'S SHORT story "The Purple Wig," the Earl of Exmoor tells Father Brown that if he removes his wig, no one will be able to bear the horror concealed under it. In fact, what the earl is concealing under his wig is a guilty secret, and he's trying to use fear to prevent Father Brown from exposing his lie. But Father Brown refuses to be intimidated. "If the devil tells you something is too fearful to look at, look at it. If he says something is too terrible to hear, hear it. If you think some truth unbearable, bear it."*

In John 8:44 Jesus called Satan the father of lies, that is, the source of every lie. Everything Satan says is a lie, because lies are his native language. He uses lies to try to intimidate us into not doing what God wants us to. *You can't do that, it's too hard. You're too young. You're too old.* If we believe that, it will block us from having the abundant life that Jesus came for us to have. Paul wrote to Timothy, "God did not give us a spirit of timidity but a spirit of power and love and self-control" (2 Tim 1:7 RSV). He was encouraging a nervous Timothy not to let fear keep him from standing by Paul when Paul was in trouble. We don't have to allow fear to stop us either. God is with us and will help us do what he wants us to do. This is the only reason given in the Bible why we shouldn't fear: God is with us. "I will fear no evil, for you are with me" (Ps 23:4 NIV)

Let's not be frightened by Satan's lies.

---

* Chesterton, "Purple Wig," 256-67.

Today's Reading: 2 Cor 5:17–18

More Lies

YESTERDAY WE THOUGHT ABOUT how Satan uses lies to intimidate us into not doing what God wants us to do. He also tells other lies, lies that have to do with who we are. These are Satan's more "theological" lies. *God doesn't love you* (for the truth, see, e.g., John 3:16; 1 John 3:1). *God won't forgive you for what you did* (for the truth, see, e.g., 1 John 1:9; 2 Cor 5:17). *You'll never change and be a good Christian* (for the truth, see 2 Cor 5:21; Phil 1:6).

Satan wants us to believe his lies about who we are, because believing them will get our focus onto ourselves and our faults rather than on Jesus. What's true of us in Christ is true of us *in Christ*. These things are true of us positionally, even if they aren't true of us physically. They're true of us because we're in Christ, whether or not they manifest themselves in our lives as much as we'd like them to. They're true because of him, not because of us. Knowing who we are in Christ will help us deal with the lies that Satan tells us. If he can keep us from believing what God says about us, that will keep us from opposing Satan and being effective for God.

There's only one thing that can overcome Satan's lies, and that's God's truth. God's word, the Bible, is truth (John 17:17). Let's learn from God's word who we are in Christ, so we can use it to defend ourselves against Satan's lies.

Father, thank you for who I am in Christ. I am who I am because he is who he is. Help me remember who I am in Christ, so I won't believe Satan's lies about me.

Today's Reading: John 10:7–9, 27–29

In His Hand

I SOMETIMES GET CALLS ON the Prayer Line from Christians who think that they've lost their salvation because they've sinned. But that's a lie from the enemy. We can't lose our salvation as easily as I lose my gloves!

In John 10:27–29, Jesus said that he knows his sheep, whom the Father has given him, and no one can snatch them out of his hand. Our salvation is not about us holding on to Jesus and trying not to lose our grip. If it were, that would mean that our salvation depends on us, not on him. But our salvation is about Jesus holding on to us. And he never loses his grip. If you're born again, you're one of Jesus' sheep, and he has you firmly in his grip. No one can snatch you out of his hand, and you can't accidentally fall out of his hand either. The Father who gave Jesus his sheep is greater than all, and the sheep are secure. That's why Jesus' half-brother Jude could end his letter with, "To him who is able to keep you from stumbling and to present you before his glorious presence without fault and with great joy . . . be glory, majesty, power and authority, through Jesus Christ our Lord, before all ages, now and forevermore!" (Jude 24–25 NIV).

We all slip up and sin sometimes. But that doesn't mean we've lost our salvation. That's what Jesus meant when he said, "Those who have had a bath need only to wash their feet; their whole body is clean" (John 13:10 NIV). When we stumble, Jesus our Advocate speaks on our behalf before the Father (1 John 2:1–2). We are secure, now and for eternity.

The Good Shepherd holds his sheep securely in his hand.

Today's Reading: Mark 6:35–44

"What's That in Your Hand?"

IT HAD BEEN A LONG hot day of teaching and ministry in the Galilean wilderness, and evening was coming. So Jesus' disciples suggested to him that he dismiss the people, so they could get something to eat. But Jesus challenged them, "*You* give them something to eat" (verse 37). They knew they didn't have nearly enough to feed the hungry crowd. All they had was five small loaves of bread and two fish. But when they brought them to Jesus, he multiplied them until there was more than enough for five thousand men, plus women and children (Matt 14:21).

There's a well-known story in the Old Testament that makes the same point. When God called Moses to lead Israel, Moses hesitated, giving several reasons why he wasn't up to the job. But God asked, "What is that in your hand?" What was in Moses' hand was an ordinary shepherd's staff (Exod 4:1–5). But it became "the rod of God," which Moses used to do many miracles.

Moses and the disciples offered God what they had, and he used it to do far more than they could have done themselves. The same is true of us. If we offer God what we have, he'll multiply it. What we have might not seem like much to us, but the fact that we offer it makes it precious to God. It doesn't matter if we have only a little to offer. What we offer to God becomes a seed that he uses to produce a crop, for his glory. We can trust him to use what we give him. All we have to do is to make ourselves available to God, and trust him for the rest.

If we offer God what we have, he'll multiply it.

Today's Reading: Gal 5:16–25

Jekyll and Hyde, Spirit and Flesh

I WAS SURPRISED TO FIND Robert Louis Stevenson's *Dr. Jekyll and Mr. Hyde* in the children's section of my local public library. This short novel (published 1886) is packed with some very grown-up ideas! There are some important spiritual lessons to be learned from this story.

Dr. Henry Jekyll is a well-respected, fifty-year-old London physician. But he's having what we would now call a mid-life crisis: he wants to indulge his passions as he did in his wild youth, without any hits to his reputation. He develops a drug which allows him to separate his evil side (whom he names Edward Hyde) from his good side. As Hyde, he can do whatever he wants, without suffering any scandal or qualms of conscience. But it all goes wrong: at first Jekyll can control Hyde, but eventually Hyde comes to control Jekyll. Jekyll is finally able to destroy Hyde, but only at the cost of his own life.*

In Christian terms, Jekyll wants to indulge his flesh without having any consequences. But that, as Jekyll finds out, is impossible. We may start out in control of the flesh, but it doesn't want to be controlled. And eventually it will control us. That's why Paul warns, "Make no provision for the flesh, to gratify its desires" (Rom 13:14 RSV). When the New Testament talks about the flesh, it doesn't mean the physical body, but the part of human nature which rebels against God. We can't deal with the flesh on our own, we need God's help. The only way for us to deal with the flesh is to live according to the Spirit, that is, to live under the Holy Spirit's guidance and control.

Let's live by the Spirit, not by the flesh.

---

* Stevenson, *Jekyll and Hyde*.

Today's Reading: Rom 8:28

No TARDIS Required

THE LONG-RUNNING BRITISH TV series *Doctor Who* is about a man who travels around in his time machine, the TARDIS. In the TARDIS the Doctor can go anywhere in time and space; but there are rules, even for time travellers. The First Law of Time forbids going back in time and changing one's own life. The Doctor has done things that he regrets, but he can't go back and change his own past.

We can't travel back in time and change our past either. We've all made mistakes. Many of us have been hurt and shamed by other people. But here's the good news: the past can't be changed, but it can be redeemed. God can redeem the past, bring good out of it. Paul wrote, "We know that in all things God works for the good of those who love him, who have been called according to his purpose" (Rom. 8:28 NIV). This doesn't mean that all things are good, but that God takes bad things and brings good out of them. Joseph told his brothers, "You intended to harm me, but God intended it for good" (Gen. 50:20 NIV). Joseph's brothers mistreated him, but God used that to put Joseph into a position where he could save them, and a lot of other people, from dying in a famine.

We don't need a time machine to deal with the painful things in our past. God can make them worthwhile by bringing something good out of them. Our pain doesn't have to be wasted; if we give it to God, it won't be.

Father, you know what's in my past. I give the hurt to you so you can redeem it and bring good out of the bad things that happened.

Today's Reading: Isa 30:20–22

Lane-Departure Warning

RECENTLY I HAD OCCASION to rent a car, and the car I rented was equipped with a lane-departure warning. A lane-departure warning is an alarm that goes off if a driver starts to drift out of their own lane. It warns the driver to get back on track before they have a collision.

In Isa 30:20–22 God promises his people that he will give them a lane-departure warning. He promises that he will be our teacher and warn us when we start drifting away from the lane of his truth. This promise has been fulfilled. God made himself visible in Jesus, the greatest teacher of all time. When Jesus returned to heaven, God sent the Holy Spirit to be our teacher and to guide us into all the truth (John 14:26; 16:13). The Spirit is one of God's lane-departure warnings. He'll let us know if we're starting to drift into wrong doctrine, wrong ideas or wrong attitudes. God's other lane-departure warning is his written word. The Bible tells us what behaviors and attitudes are right, and warns of sins to avoid. That's why the psalmist could say, "Your word is a lamp for my feet, a light on my path" (Ps 119:105 NIV). Our part is to listen for the voice of conviction, and, when we hear it, to course-correct back to where we should be, with God's help. If we listen to the Spirit and the word, we can avoid the hurt that can come from getting off-track spiritually. They'll help us stay safely in the lane of God's truth.

Father, thank you for giving me the Holy Spirit and your word to warn me when I start to go off-course spiritually. Help me hear and respond to him. In Jesus' name, amen.

Today's Reading: Eph 4:32—5:2

Like Father, Like Child

A MAN TIGHTENED THE SCREW on the knob on a cupboard door using a screwdriver. A few feet away, a little boy twisted his pointing finger against the door on another cupboard. The man was pleased and amused to see his son trying to do as his father was doing.

The peoples of Bible times didn't have our saying, "Like father, like son," but they would have understood it. A son was expected to learn his father's trade, and take over his business in due time (James and John were fishermen like their father Zebedee; Matt 4:21). Girls learned from their mothers how to keep house; Jewish girls were expected to learn from their mothers how to cook according to the Mosaic food laws.

We are children of our heavenly Father, and he wants us to do as he does. Jesus made it clear during his ministry that he was doing as his Father did (John 5:17-21). And he said that we should follow his example of humble service to one another (John 13:12-15). Paul may have had this in mind when he wrote, "Be imitators of me, as I am of Christ" (1 Cor 11:1 NIV). And he makes the same point in Phil 2:5-11: we should have the same humble attitude that Jesus showed by his incarnation and death. Perhaps this is one reason why Jesus became flesh. How could we imitate a God whom we couldn't see? But we did see Jesus, and he taught us about his Father, and showed us how to walk in his ways (John 1:14,18). Let's be imitators of our Father, like good children.

Jesus, help us to be imitators of you and walk in your ways, just as you did what you saw your Father doing.

Today's Reading: Ps 34:9–10

The Little Things

KAREN WAS ABOUT TO leave her home when she found that she had misplaced her car keys. Then she remembered her pastor saying that God cares about everything that we care about. So she prayed, "God, you know where my keys are. Please help me find them." She began to look for her keys, and sure enough, a few minutes later she found them. She went on her way rejoicing in God's love and care.

There's no issue so small that God doesn't care about it, and no issue so big that he can't handle it. Because he loves us, he's concerned about everything that concerns us. We can go to him with even things that might seem small and insignificant, because he cares about those things and will help us with them. Whether it's lost keys, lost eyeglasses or lost dentures, God cares. He won't think we're foolish if we bring these little things to him. When we do that, it shows our trust in him, and he delights in that. He also delights in showing his loving care for us by helping us with these things. Just as loving parents delight in doing small things for their children, our loving heavenly Father delights in taking care of the small things for his children. Peter wrote that we can cast all our cares on the Lord, because he cares about us (1 Pet 5:7). And in Ps 34:10 David wrote, "The young lions suffer want and hunger; but those who seek the Lord lack no good thing" (RSV). So we don't need to hesitate to come to God for help with the little things.

There's no issue so small that God doesn't care about it. He's concerned about everything that concerns us.

Today's Reading: Eph 1:5–8

Letting Go of Guilt

THE BBC-TV SERIES *FATHER BROWN* is based on G.K. Chesterton's priest-detective. In the season 2 episode "The Maddest of All," Father Brown encounters a doctor who runs a mental hospital, who is doing experiments on his patients. It turns out that the doctor wants to heal his brain-injured son. The young man was injured in an auto collision that killed his mother; the doctor was driving, and feels responsible for his wife's death and his son's injury. Father Brown finally tells the doctor, "Let go of your guilt."*

This issue of guilt arises frequently in ministry. The enemy is very good at keeping people trapped in guilt over things that God has forgiven. But we don't have to believe his lies. One of the enemy's lies is that we've gone too far, that what we've done is too bad for God to forgive. But this is arrogance. Can we really do anything that's too big for God to handle? There's nothing that God will not forgive if we genuinely repent. Another lie is that God won't forgive us because we don't deserve to be forgiven. But God doesn't forgive us because we deserve it; he forgives us because of what Jesus did on the cross. We can't earn forgiveness. All we can do is to open our hearts and receive forgiveness as a gift from God. That can be difficult, because there's something in human nature which wants to earn what it gets. But we can't earn the forgiveness that God wants to give us. All we can do, all we need to do, is to receive by faith the gift that Jesus has already paid for with his blood.

We can live in the forgiveness that Jesus died for us to have.

* Carter, *Father Brown*, "Maddest."

Today's Reading: John 18:4–9

Examples for Tough Times

MANY YEARS AGO, in Bible school, I learned a lesson I'll never forget, and it didn't come from the classroom. I'd been going through a difficult time, and one day a fellow student left me an unsigned note: "This is to let you know that someone has you in prayer." I didn't find out who it was until a few weeks later—by which time this student had taken her own life. I knew that she'd struggled with depression, but I had no idea how serious her problem was. In the midst of all her pain, she took a few minutes do something for me. It was an example I won't forget, even if I haven't always gone and done likewise.

This is also the example that Jesus gave his disciples. At the Last Supper, he took the time to reassure and instruct his disciples, in spite of what he must have been feeling (John 14—16). When he was arrested, he made sure they were safe (John 18:8). While he was on the cross, he made sure that his mother would be cared for (John 19:26-27). Similarly Paul, on his last voyage to Jerusalem, met with leaders of the churches he'd founded, comforting and instructing those he would leave behind (Acts 20:17—21:14). This example is for us too. When we're going through tough times, the best thing we can do for ourselves is to think about others. To do things for others, as we're able to. That isn't easy, and I haven't always done it as I should. But it shows that we trust God to take care of our problems.

When we're going through tough times, the best thing we can do for ourselves is to do something for others.

Today's Reading: 1 John 2:15–17

Here, On the Way to There

IN SIR ARTHUR CONAN DOYLE'S "The Adventure of the Creeping Man" (originally published 1923) Sherlock Holmes encounters a man who wants to get his "mojo" back. Sixty-one-year-old professor Presbury, a widower, has a brilliant career and a widespread reputation. But he has become infatuated with his colleague's young daughter. In an attempt to regain his virility, he begins to take a drug made from monkeys (we're safe in assuming that it contains testosterone from male monkeys). Not surprisingly, something goes wrong. Presbury begins to act like a monkey, climbing the ivy on the walls of his house and teasing his dog. The dog finally attacks him, and only the quick action of Holmes, Dr. Watson, and Presbury's assistant prevent him from being killed. Holmes says that the root of the problem is the professor's sensual, worldly desires, and says, "The spiritual would not avoid the call to something higher."*

This world, this life, is not all there is. As has often been said, Christians should live this life in view of the next. There's no need for us to completely ignore the pleasures and beauties of creation; God created the world, and called it "very good" (Gen 1:31). Nor should we ignore the needs of this world, if there's something we can do to help (Jas 2:15–16). But our main focus should be the next world, not this one. John warns believers not to love this world (i.e. this present-age system that is opposed to God) because what comes from this world doesn't come from God (1 John 2:15–16). We're citizens of heaven (Phil 3:20) so while we're here on earth, let's live like citizens of heaven should.

Let's live our lives "here" in view of the next life "there."

---

* Doyle, *Complete Sherlock Holmes*, 1070–83.

Today's Reading: Matt 10:2–4

A Motley Crew

WE CAN MISS WHAT a mixed group the Twelve were. But the list starts with Simon Peter, the impulsive man of action; James son of Zebedee, the fisherman-turned-administrator who led the Jerusalem church in its earliest beginnings; and his contemplative younger brother John. The next group includes Philip, whose Greek name indicates that he may have been of Gentile descent; then come Thomas, whose faith was sometimes weak (see John 11:16; 20:24–25) and Matthew, whose job as a tax collector hints at his pro-Roman politics. The list concludes with Simon the Zealot, whose nickname hints that he was an Israelite nationalist; and Judas Iscariot, the group's treasurer, who would turn traitor. Looking at this partial list, it's easy to see the possibilities for conflict. We know that they argued repeatedly about which of them was the greatest (see Mark 9:34; Luke 9:46; 22:24). But did Peter ever tell John to stop contemplating and do something? Did John answer that Peter should slow down and think before he acted? Did the fishermen-disciples ever complain to Matthew about business taxes? Did Matthew and Simon the Zealot ever argue about politics? When it comes down to it, there was only one thing that all the Twelve had in common, and that was Jesus himself.

It's the same with the church today. We each have different characters and physical characteristics; we come from all cultures and all socioeconomic strata. The only thing that we all share is "one hope. . . one Lord, one faith, one baptism, one God and Father of us all, who is above all and through all and in all" (Eph 4:4–6 RSV).

Lord Jesus, head of the body of Christ, help me to respect and love Christians who are different from me.

Today's Reading: Num 13:1–2; 26–33

Tricked

J.R.R. TOLKEIN'S *THE LORD OF THE RINGS* is one of my favorite novels. There are many theological lessons to be learned from this story, but one of them caught my attention only recently. Two characters, Saruman and Denethor, are leaders of the West who go over to the side of the enemy, Sauron. Saruman comes to think that they can't beat Sauron, so joining him is the only way to survive. Denethor, his army being driven back, gives in to despair. But here's the important thing: Sauron (whom Gandalf on one occasion calls Sauron the Deceiver) brings them over to his side by tricking them into seeing what he wants them to see. Thus he convinces them that he's stronger than he really is.*

This is what happened to the Israelites in Num 13. They were on the border of the Promised Land. But when they saw the enemies facing them, all they could see was how strong those enemies were. Only Joshua and Caleb could see that going before them was a God who was stronger than their enemies. Because of this an entire generation of Israelites didn't get into the Promised Land.

We also have an enemy, Satan, the father of lies (John 8:44). He'll try to trick us into believing that he's stronger than he really is, that he can't be beaten. But Jesus has already beaten him, two thousand years ago at Calvary. If we focus on the enemy, we give him more power and authority than he really has. We'll have to fight some battles with Satan, but Jesus has already won the war. We can't beat Satan on our own, but we aren't on our own; Jesus is with us.

Satan is a defeated foe; Jesus has defeated him.

---

* Tolkien, *Rings*, 259, 755–757.

Today's Reading: Ps 150

Make a Joyful Noise

I COME FROM A MUSICAL FAMILY. Four generations of my family have been musicians, whether as professionals, semi-professionals, or amateurs like myself. And a fifth generation is arising to take its place in this family tradition–some of my nieces and nephews are musical. Perhaps it's not surprising, then, that music has always been an important part of worship for me.

Music has been important to the church since her earliest days. In fact, scholars are generally agreed that several passages in the New Testament are probably hymns that the writer is quoting (see Phil 2:5–11; Col 1:15–20; Heb 1:1–3; 1 Pet 2:21–25).* The earliest Christians sang regularly (Eph 5:19; 1 Cor 14:26; Jas 5:13). And Paul and Silas sang hymns to encourage themselves when they were in prison (Acts 16:25). Scripture indicates that music was an important part of Jewish worship (see, e.g. 1 Chron 15:16–24; 25:1–7; Ps 92:1–4) so it's not surprising that the early Christians brought music into their own worship. The Greeks and Romans also sang hymns to their gods, so Gentile Christians had no problem joining in the music of the church, in worship of Jesus. So it's fitting that the church should continue to make music today. I for one am glad that the church uses different styles of music, too, whether hymns, gospel, contemporary, or urban hip-hop. There's room enough for all, especially since some people will be reached by one type of music and some by another. It's sad when music becomes a cause of strife between Christians. Music and worship should unite us, not divide us. Let's join together and "make a joyful noise to the LORD" (Ps 100:1 RSV).

Thank you Father for giving us the gift of music to praise you with.

---

* This list from Jipp, "Hymns."

Today's Reading: Matt 1:20–21

Names of Jesus

THE NAMES AND TITLES given to Jesus tell us something about who he is and what he has done. The name Jesus itself means "God saves;" he was called that because he would save his people from their sins (verse 21). Here are just a few of his names and titles:

- He is Immanuel, which means "God with us" (Matt 1:23) because he is with us always (Matt 28:20).
- He is the Son of man (Matt 9:6) because he is fully human as well as fully divine.
- He is the Son of God (Matt 16:16) because he is fully divine as well as fully human.
- He is the son of David (Mark 10:47–48) because he's descended from King David in his earthly lineage. This is a royal title, which hints that Jesus is king of Israel (John 1:49).
- He is the Word, God's ultimate expression of himself (John 1:1–2, 18).
- He is the Lamb of God (John 1:29, 36) because he is the atoning sacrifice for our sins.
- He is the bread of life (John 6:35) because he provides us with spiritual sustenance.
- He is the good shepherd (John 10:11–16) because he cares for his sheep.
- He is our peace, because he has broken down dividing walls of racial hostility (Eph 2:14).
- He is our high priest, who represents us to God and represents God to us (Heb 3:1; 4:14–15)
- He is our advocate (1 John 2:1) our defence lawyer before the Father when we sin.
- Last but by no means least, he has the name which is above every name: Jesus is Lord (Phil 2:11).

No one name can fully convey who Jesus is. But his names help us understand him.

> The names of Jesus help us understand who he is and what he has done.

Today's Reading: 1 Cor 9:24–27

High-Performance

AS I WRITE THIS, the eyes of the world are on Beijing for the 2022 Winter Olympics. There were four major athletic competitions in Paul's day: the Olympics, the Isthmian Games, the Nemean Games, and the Pythian Games. Olympic champions were crowned with a wreath of olive leaves, winners in the Isthmian Games got one of pine, winners in the Pythian Games got one of bay laurel leaves, and winners in the Nemean Games got one of wild-celery leaves. Sports were as much a part of life in the first century as they are in the twenty-first, so it's no surprise that Paul refers to sports a number of times in his letters.

Elite athletes take their sport seriously, and they train hard to get ready for competition. They spend hours exercising, they're careful about what they eat and they make sure they get enough sleep. In 1 Cor 9: 24–27, Paul's point is that Christians should be as serious about their faith as athletes are about their training. After all, the prize we're running for isn't a wreath that will wither away, or even a medal, but an eternal one. All the more reason, then, for us to train to be the best we can be.

So how do we become high-performance Christians? It involves the discipline of spending time with God in prayer and Bible study, and with our teammates, our brothers and sisters in Christ. It also involves the discipline of saying No to our flesh. It isn't easy. But we have teammates to cheer us on, and our Coach, the Holy Spirit, to teach us and empower us. With their help, we can be the best we can be.

Holy Spirit, our Coach, help us to be high-performance Christians.

Today's Reading: Phil 4:6–7

Peace

THESE ARE STRESSFUL TIMES. Most of us have something in our lives to worry about. Finances, family matters, physical problems . . . the list can go on and on. And if our own affairs aren't enough, a look at the news can give us national or international matters to worry about. So how do we stop it all from getting to us?

We have such a great need for peace right now, and God's people don't have far to look for it. God has already given us his peace. This is what Jesus meant when he said, "Peace I leave with you; my peace I give to you; not as the world gives do I give to you. Let not your hearts be troubled, neither let them be afraid" (John 14:27 RSV). The Greek word translated "leave" can be used of inheritance—peace is the legacy that Jesus has left us as his disciples. Peace is also a fruit of the Spirit (Gal 5:22), a natural result of the Spirit's operation in our lives. So as believers we have peace, and all the other fruit of the Spirit, even if we only have it in seed-form. For these two reasons, believers have God's peace. So how do we access this peace? Paul gives us a clue in Phil 4:6–7. If we give our worries to God in prayer, his peace will guard our hearts and minds. Similarly Isa 26:3 says, "You will keep in perfect peace those whose minds are steadfast [i.e., focused on God], because they trust in you" (NIV). This putting things into God's hands isn't always easy, because it means giving him control of the situation. But it's the way to have peace.

We have God's peace; all we have to do is access it.

Today's Reading: Gal 3:26–28

Our Last Battlefield?

IN THE CLASSIC *STAR TREK* episode "Let That Be Your Last Battlefield," Captain Kirk and his crew encounter Lokai, an activist from the planet Cherron, and Commissioner Bele, a law enforcement officer who has pursued Lokai for fifty thousand years. At first the *Enterprise* crew can't see any difference between them, until Bele points out that he and his people are black on the right side and white on the left, while Lokai and his people are white on the right side and black on the left.* That the theme of this issue is race is clear—so much so that some reviewers have faulted the episode for heavy-handedness. We can't fully discuss here the issue of race, or the damage that racism has done over the last four centuries. But watching this episode led me to ask what the Bible says about race.

We're all descended from one pair, Adam and Eve, and all made in God's image (Gen 1:26). God loves all people equally, believers and nonbelievers alike. He doesn't play favourites (Deut 10:17; Acts 10:34; Rom 2:11; Eph 6:9). With his blood Jesus has "purchased for God persons from every tribe and language and people and nation." (Rev 5:9 NIV). That's why Paul could write, "There is neither Jew nor Gentile . . . for you are all one in Christ Jesus" (verse 28 RSV). And John sees a vision of the future in which "a great multitude that no one could count, from every nation, tribe, people and language, stand[s] before the throne and before the Lamb" (Rev 7:9 NIV). All this suggests to me that the church should be a leader in showing racial equality.

Let's be an example to the world in showing God's love to all people, whatever their skin color.

---

* Taylor, *Trek*, Last Battlefield."

Today's Reading: Jer 31:31–34

Change of Law, Change of Heart

IN THE PAST SEVERAL months there has been a lot of discussion about race, and about the need for laws to protect Black, Indigenous, Asian, and Muslim people. There's a call to change the law, and change is needed. But is the law all that needs to change?

The law governs people's actions. It says, "If you do such-and-such, you'll pay the penalty." But in order to end racial prejudice, what needs to change is people's hearts and minds. And the law can't do that. Only God, acting through the Holy Spirit, can do that.

This an important theme in both the Old and New Testaments. The unredeemed heart is thoroughly deceitful and corrupt (Jer 17:9). This is the real root of all wrong attitudes and actions (Matt 15:18–19). And there's nothing we humans can do to change that, as Paul points out (Rom 7:14–23). But God can, and will, do for us what we can't do for ourselves. He will replace our stony hearts with hearts of flesh that will obey him (Ezek 11:19–20). God promised that he would make a new covenant with Israel, writing it on their minds and hearts, so that all God's people would know him (Jer 31:31–34). This is the promise of the new covenant in Christ.

The classic *Star Trek* episode "Let That Be Your Last Battlefield" ends with Bele chasing Lokai on their home planet. Cherron is long dead, its cities burned, its people destroyed. The *Enterprise* crew observe sadly that all Lokai and Bele have left is their hate.[*] Can we do better? We must do better, and with God's help, we can.

In order to end hate crimes, hatred must end. The heart must be changed as well as the law.

---

[*] Taylor, *Trek*, "Last Battlefield."

Today's Reading: 2 Cor 12:7–10

His Power, Our Weakness

MANY TIMES IN MINISTRY I have encountered people who are suffering from long-term physical or emotional problems. When such problems go on for a long time, the duration can cause its own problems in addition to the problems caused by the illness itself. People can get worn down simply by how long an illness goes on.

The apostle Paul suffered from what he calls "a thorn in the flesh" (2 Cor 12:7). He doesn't specify what it was; apparently his readers knew. Most likely it was some kind of physical problem. Paul prayed repeatedly for healing, but he didn't get healed. Instead God told him, "My grace is sufficient for you, for my power is made perfect in weakness" (verse 9 RSV). In other words, God promised Paul that he would give Paul the grace to cope with his problem. That would show God's power even more than a miraculous healing. Paul was content with this, because his priority was that God be glorified. In his weakness, God would make him strong.

If you're struggling with long-term physical or emotional problems, know that God's promise to you is the same as his promise to Paul. If God doesn't heal you, he'll give you the grace and strength you need to cope with your problems. Your weakness will be the very thing that shows God's power the most. In your weakness, God will give you greater strength than you could ever have on your own. This will be a testimony to others of what God can do. His strength is made perfect in your weakness, for when you are weak, then you are strong.

If God doesn't heal us, he'll give us the grace and strength we need to cope with our problems.

Today's Reading: Heb 12:1–2

Running to Win

THE RUNNER TRIPPED OVER a fallen competitor and fell, but got up and kept running. And powered past the other competitors, one at a time, to win. But it wasn't a scene from the movie *Chariots of Fire*.* It was the Tokyo 2020 Olympics. Sifan Hassan of the Netherlands fell in her heat of the women's 1500 metres, but won (she went on to win the bronze medal).

The New Testament pictures the Christian life as a race. The writer of Hebrews encourages his readers, "Let us throw off everything that hinders and the sin that so easily entangles. And let us run with perseverance the race marked out for us" Heb 12:1 NIV). Wrong attitudes like pride, bitterness and unforgiveness, or fear can weigh us down. Being distracted by worldly cares and pleasures can slow us down too. All these things get our focus onto ourselves and our circumstances instead of onto Jesus. It also slows us down if we get tangled up in sin (the image is of a runner's clothes tangling their legs so that they trip). The way we avoid these dangers is to keep our eyes on Jesus. Only then can we persevere and run the race that God has set before us (verse 2). Similarly Paul says, "Do you not know that in a race all the runners run, but only one gets the prize? Run in such a way as to get the prize" (1 Cor 9:24 NIV). With God's help, let's get rid of anything that would slow us down or trip us up, so we can run our Christian race to win.

Father, I want to run my race to win. Help me set aside anything that would slow me down or entangle me.

* Hudson, *Chariots*.

Today's Reading: Ps 19:7–13

A Safe Place

I HAD BEGUN VACUUMING and washing my floor when I realized that my cat, Cleopatra, was sitting on my bed. I said to her, "Stay there, Cleo, that's a good place for you to be." If she stayed on the bed, she'd avoid getting her feet wet.

There's a safe place for us to stay in life, too, and that's within the boundaries of God's word. If we follow the instructions for life laid out in Scripture, it will keep us from hurting ourselves emotionally and spiritually. This is what Ps 119:9 means when it says that the way to keep one's life pure is to live according to God's word. And in Ps 19:7–13, David exults in how beneficial to us God's laws are. They refresh the soul, make uneducated people wise, and they give joy to the heart and light to the eyes.

The book of Proverbs is full of practical advice on what living according to God's word looks like. It gives positive instruction (see, e.g., Prov 16:1–24; 21:21–31) and warns of pitfalls to avoid (see, e.g., Prov 4:14–19; 5:21—6:19). Similarly in the New Testament, the letters of Paul and the others tell us what life in Christ looks like. In 1 and 2 Corinthians Paul deals with problems in that church, thus showing us what to avoid. The other letters tell us how to live the way God wants us to.

God isn't a spoilsport. His rules for us are for our good. So when God says No to something, he's really saying, "Don't do that, you'll hurt yourself if you do." The best way to live is the way God says to.

Within the boundaries of God's word is the safest place for us to live.

Today's Reading: John 10:2–4

The Star-Shepherd

ONE OF MY FAVOURITE Old Testament verses is Isa 40:26: "Lift up your eyes and look to the heavens: Who created all these? He who brings out the starry host one by one and calls forth each of them by name. Because of his great power and mighty strength, not one of them is missing" (NIV).

This verse always reminds me of God as Shepherd, bringing the stars out at night as a shepherd brings his sheep out to pasture. In accordance with ancient Mediterranean custom, the shepherd knows each member of the flock, and calls them by name. Because of the Star-Shepherd's great power, not one of his flock is missing.

I wonder if Jesus was thinking of this verse when he said, "He who enters by the door is the shepherd of the sheep . . . he calls his own sheep by name and leads them out. When he has brought out all his own, he goes before them, and the sheep follow him, for they know his voice" (John 10:2–4 RSV).

If he can do that for the stars, he can do it for us. Just as the stars are his flock, so are we. He knows each of us individually. He knows our fears, our hopes, and our desires. And because of his great power, he keeps us safe.

The Shepherd of the stars is our Shepherd too. If he can bring the stars out every night and keep them safe by his great power, he can do that for us. Whatever hard times might come into our lives, he'll bring us safely through them. The Star-Shepherd cares about us, and he takes care of us. We're safe in his keeping.

The LORD is my shepherd; I shall not want. (Ps 23:1 RSV)

Today's Reading: Eph 4:30

Sealed with the Spirit

PIERRE, A SKILLED HOCKEY player, was proud to play for McMaster University's team. Which was why he wore a T-shirt that said, "Property of McMaster University Athletics Dept." It was a sign proclaiming his allegiance. As Christians, we also wear a sign: the New Testament says that we are "sealed with the [Holy] Spirit" (Eph 1:13; 4:30). But what does this mean?

In ancient times, a seal was a symbol stamped onto a blob of soft wax or clay which was then pressed onto an object to mark that object as someone's private property. But there's more: the seal was backed by the authority of the person whose seal it was. There would be consequences for anyone who tampered with it. A modern equivalent would be our PRIVATE PROPERTY NO TRESSPASSING sign, which indicates that a place is someone's private possession, and anyone who goes there without the owner's permission will suffer the penalty of the law.

The Holy Spirit in us is God's mark on us, the sign that we are his. But there's more: just as a NO TRESSPASSING sign means that a property is protected by the law, the seal of the Holy Spirit means that God's protection is on us. The enemy may attack us, but "he who is in [us] is greater than he who is in the world" (1 John 4:4 RSV). God is stronger than the enemy, and when the enemy attacks us, God will help us deal with it. We who are sealed with the Holy Spirit don't need to be afraid of the enemy, because we are God's private property and he will protect us.

The Holy Spirit in us is a sign that we are God's private property and he will protect us.

Today's Reading: Gal 6:7–9

"Stick-to-it-iveness"

My father approved of a person with what he called "stick-to-it-iveness." A person with "stick-to-it-iveness" doesn't give up when things get tough. They finish what they've started, and do what they say they'll do. They persist. What my father called 'stick-to-it-iveness," the Bible calls faithfulness.

The ultimate example of faithfulness, of course, is God. A famous verse about God's faithfulness is Num 23:19, "God is not human, that he should lie, not a human being, that he should change his mind. Does he speak and then not act? Does he promise and not fulfill?" (NIV). Equally famous is 1 Thess 5:24, "He who calls you is faithful, and he will do it." (RSV). In the context, this refers to God's ability to keep those whom he has called strong in the faith until the end.

God wants his people to follow his example. Ps 15:4 says that the person "who keeps an oath even when it hurts, and does not change their mind" (NIV) may live in God's holy dwelling; this refers to the person who keeps a commitment even when they find out it's inconvenient to do so. But this kind of faithfulness isn't always easy. It involves persistence. It means not giving up in difficult situations. That's why Paul encourages his readers, "Let us not become weary in doing good, for at the proper time we will reap a harvest if we do not give up." (verse 9 NIV). In the context, Paul is talking about sowing and reaping. If we keep sowing the seed of right behavior, we'll eventually reap a harvest of blessing. We may note that Paul doesn't give a specific time limit for God to reward us; he just says, "at the proper time."

Father, help me follow your example of faithfulness.

Today's Reading: Esth 4:12–14

For Such a Time as This

IN J.R.R. TOLKIEN'S *THE LORD OF THE RINGS*, an important conversation takes place early in the story. When Gandalf first tells Frodo about the Ring and its history, Frodo is alarmed and uncertain if he can handle the situation. He says that he wishes that these things had not happened in his time. Gandalf answers, "So do I, and so do all who live to see such times. But that is not for them to decide. All we have to decide is what to do with the time that is given us."* Gandalf is certain that Frodo was meant to have the ring, and not by its evil maker.**

Queen Esther must have felt the same way as Frodo—frightened and unsure if she could do anything to save her people. She knew her life would be at risk. When she hesitated to get involved, her uncle Mordecai answered, "Do not think that because you are in the king's house you alone of all the Jews will escape . . . And who knows but that you have come to your royal position for such a time as this?" (Esth 4:13–14 NIV). Mordecai believed that God had put Esther into a position where she could do something about the crisis.

Like Frodo and Esther, we have been placed where we are, when we are, for a reason. God has put us in place so that he can use us to accomplish his purposes in the world. But this is no guarantee of a trouble-free life. We have to choose whether we hide in a corner or stand up and take the risk that comes with getting involved.

God has placed us where we are, when we are, for a reason.

---

* Tolkien, *Rings*, 51.
** Tolkien, *Rings*, 56.

Today's Reading: Col 1:15–20

The Theory of Everything

THE MOVIE *THE THEORY OF EVERYTHING* is about physicist Stephen Hawking (1942–2018). Hawking sought "a unifying theory—a single equation that explains everything in the universe."* Hawking never did find his equation, because, sadly, he was looking in the wrong direction. What explains everything in the universe isn't a theory or an equation but a person.

The Bible makes it clear that Jesus is the agent through whom God created all things. John writes, "Through him all things were made; without him nothing was made that has been made . . . the world was made through him" (John 1:3, 10 NIV). And the writer of Hebrews says that God's Son is the one "through whom [God] also created the universe" (Heb 1:2 NIV). But Jesus isn't only God's agent in creation in the past. He is also God's agent in maintenance in the present, "upholding the universe by his word of power" (Heb 1:3 RSV). As Paul puts it, "[Jesus] is before all things, and in him all things hold together" (Col 1:17 NIV). (The last part of this verse is the motto of McMaster Divinity College, where I trained.) By his word he created the universe, and by his word he keeps it from falling apart. He who created the universe has been upholding it ever since, and he will continue to uphold it until the end.

We can trust him who upholds all things to keep all things in order. When things seem to us to be falling apart, that's just how it seems from our point of view. We don't see the whole picture. He's in control, he'll work things out.

What explains, and upholds, everything in the universe isn't a theory or an equation but a person, Jesus.

---

* Marsh, *Theory of Everything*.

Today's Reading: Rom 8:35–39

Totality Doesn't Last Forever

ON AUGUST 21, 2017, all North America was looking skyward to watch a total solar eclipse. For a few minutes, the moon came between the sun and the earth and blocked out the sun's light. Even as I was marvelling at how amazing God's creation is, I noticed something else: totality doesn't last forever. The darkness can't block out the light forever.

It's the same in our lives. Sometimes it seems like circumstances are blocking out the light of God's presence and help. It may be a serious illness, the loss of a spouse or loved one, financial hardship, or other difficult circumstance. We can be left wondering where God is, or if he's strong enough to help us. But these times don't—can't—last forever. There is no circumstance that can overcome the power of God. As the apostle Paul—who was no stranger to hard times—puts it, nothing can separate us from the love of God that is in Christ Jesus our Lord (see Rom. 8:38–39). A few verses earlier Paul asks, "Who shall separate us from the love of Christ? Shall trouble or hardship or persecution or famine or nakedness or danger or sword?" (Rom 8:35 NIV). (Interestingly, all these things had happened to Paul, except the sword. And that was to come: church tradition says that Paul was beheaded in a Roman prison.) The light shines in the darkness, and the darkness can't even understand it, let alone overcome it (John 1:5). Whatever is happening, God can, and will, bring us through it.

Father, help me to remember that the dark times are only temporary. They can't eclipse the light of your presence and help. I trust you to bring me through the darkness into the light.

Today's Reading: Heb 4:14–16

Unprecedented Christmas

Elvis Presley laments that he'll have a blue Christmas, in one of his most popular songs. For many people, a blue Christmas isn't a song but a painful reality. Christmas can be hard for those who are alone because of family situations, or physical or mental illness. This year there are those—like me—who can't be with their families for Christmas because of COVID-19. If this is your situation, know that you're not as alone as you might think.

God knows what it's like to go through hard times. To be lonely, poor, or rejected. God sent his Son Jesus as a baby, not an adult, so he would experience every facet of human existence. Jesus knows what it's like to be human, the difficulties as well as the joys, because he is fully human as well as fully divine. That's why the writer of Hebrews can say, "We do not have a high priest who is unable to sympathize with our weaknesses, but we have one who has been tempted in every way, just as we are—yet was without sin" (Heb. 4:15 NIV).

A passage of Scripture that's often read at Christmas is Matt. 1:22–23, where Matthew, quoting Isa.7:14, gives Jesus the name prophesied for him: Immanuel, which means "God with us." But there's more. Jesus himself claims this name for himself at the end of Matthew's Gospel: "Surely I am with you always, to the very end of the age" (Matt. 28:20 NIV). Jesus has fulfilled Isaiah's prophecy, and more than fulfilled it. Jesus is always with us, even when we don't feel like he's there. He is Immanuel, God with us.

Even when life is hard, we can be joyful at Christmas time, because Jesus our Immanuel has come.

Today's Reading: Jas 3:2-8

Watch Your Mouth

HUMANS HAVE SEVERAL CHARACTERISTICS that distinguish us from animals. The most important of these is speech. Animals can communicate; my cat can let me know when she wants me to feed her or pick her up and cuddle her. Animals can communicate, whether through body language or vocalizations like barking, meowing, or growling. But only humans speak using words.

This ability to use words is a characteristic that we share with God, part of being made in his image. It was by his words that God created, and still upholds, all things (Gen 1:3-24; Heb 1:3). Our words don't have quite that much power, but because we're made in the image of God, our words have power too. If you've ever persuaded someone to do something you wanted them to do, you've demonstrated that. And if you've ever talked yourself into a bad mood by complaining, you've demonstrated it too.

With this power comes responsibility. Since we can help or harm others, or ourselves, with our words, we need to watch what we say. This includes what we tell ourselves about ourselves. Let's avoid saying things like, "I'm so stupid. I'm such a sinner. I don't deserve God's blessings." And let's use our words to build up and encourage ourselves and others. James wrote that anyone who has complete control over their tongue is spiritually mature, and has control over every other area of their life as well (Jas 3:2). So maybe there are some of you who would join me in praying, with David, "Set a guard over my mouth, O Lord, keep watch over the door of my lips!" (Ps 141:3 RSV).

Father, help me use my words to encourage others and myself. Help me watch what I say.

Today's Reading: 1 John 4:8–10

To Know What Love Is

I WAS ALONE ONE EVENING when Foreigner's 1984 hit song "I Want to Know What Love Is" came on the radio. Since I was alone, I sang along. I'd heard that song before, but that evening, for the first and only time, I turned it into a heart's cry for a mate. For a godly man to share my life with. Into my mind came a vision of the cross, as if God were telling me that in the life and death of Jesus, he had shown me what real love is.

This is what John means in 1 John 4:9–10. God loves us so much that he sent his son Jesus to become one of us. And as if that weren't enough, Jesus suffered a painful and humiliating death, paying the price for our sins so that we could have eternal life (we can't fail to mention John 3:16 here, too). The apostle Paul adds more. He says that God didn't wait to send Jesus until we deserved it. Christ died for us while we were still sinners (Rom 5:8). This means that God made the first move.

There's often an element of selfishness in human love. We love someone because they can do something for us. But God's love for us isn't like that. God's love for us is to our advantage, not his. We can also say that while human love can change with circumstances, God's love for us doesn't change, because God doesn't change. God doesn't love us any less when we sin. The Bible makes it clear that God's love is unfailing (see, e.g., Pss 13:5; 33:22; Lam 3:22–23).

God has shown us what real love is, in the life and death of Jesus.

Today's Reading: Matt 5:14–16

The Whole World is Watching

"THE WHOLE WORLD IS WATCHING!" Anti-government protesters have chanted this at rallies since the 1950s. It was first used by the Civil Rights movement, and later by opponents of the war in Vietnam. Today it's frequently used at rallies. It's a reminder to governments and those in authority that what they do can't be kept secret, and wrong behavior will be exposed for all to see.

This is also true for us as Christians. The world (that is, those who are opposed to God and his kingdom) is watching us. Some of them are looking for an opportunity to take us down. Some of them are looking for an excuse to justify their own unbelief. All of them are looking to see if we really are who we say we are.

So how should we respond to this scrutiny? It's important that we live godly, authentic lives. As Paul puts it, "Be wise in the way you act toward outsiders; make the most of every opportunity. Let your conversation be always full of grace, seasoned with salt, so that you may know how to answer everyone" (Col 4:5–6 NIV). This is how we earn people's respect and win them into the kingdom. Peter writes, "Live such good lives among the pagans that, though they accuse you of doing wrong, they may see your good deeds and glorify God on the day he visits us (1 Pet 2:12 NIV). In other words, we should live such good lives that we don't give anyone any reason to accuse us of anything. Let's live rightly before the world.

The world is watching us, so let's in such a way that we earn people's respect and win them into the kingdom of God.

Today's Reading: 1 Cor 6:19-20

Bought with a Price

THE CLASSIC BRITISH TV SERIES *The Prisoner* (1967-1968) is about a senior MI6 agent who resigns after an argument with a superior. He returns to his London home, but is kidnapped and finds himself in a place known only as the Village, a place which looks like a British holiday resort but is run by people who are ruthlessly determined to find out why he resigned. Or at least, that's the surface story. But through its sixteen episodes this series raises many philosophical and theological questions that TV doesn't usually deal with.

In the series' first episode, "Arrival," the ex-agent (who is never named, and known only as "Number 6") insists, "I will not be pushed, filed, stamped, indexed, briefed, debriefed, or numbered. My life is my own."* The last part of this reminds me of part of 1 Cor 6:19-20: "You are not your own; you were bought with a price" (RSV).

When we receive Jesus as Savior, we acknowledge that God has bought and paid for us, because he paid for our redemption from our sins. Peter tells us what price God paid: "the precious blood of Christ, like that of a lamb without blemish or spot" (1 Pet 1:19 RSV). That being so, says Paul, we no longer belong to ourselves, we belong to God. It has rightly been said that when we take Jesus as our Savior, we take him as our Lord.

The Christian life is a life of obedience to God. It isn't always easy. But our Lord is loving and good, and he wants the best for us. Living under God's lordship isn't the easiest way to live, but it's the best way to live.

We don't belong to ourselves, we belong to God.

---

* Chaffey, *Prisoner*, "Arrival."

Today's Reading: John 15:1–5

Abiding in the Vine

C.S. Lewis's *THE LION, THE WITCH AND THE WARDROBE* is the second book in *The Chronicles of Narnia* series. Four English children are transported from war-torn England to the magical land of Narnia. There they meet a pair of Beavers, who tell them that their coming fulfils a prophecy: when four humans sit on thrones in the city of Cair Paravel, Aslan the great Lion will come and end the time of evil. One of the children leaves to betray the others to the evil White Witch. The other children want to look for him; Mr. Beaver says there's nothing they can do, but now that Aslan is around, something can be done.* Near the end of the book, Peter, the oldest child, leads a force into battle against the Witch and her forces; but they're losing the battle until Aslan himself arrives.** In other words, they can do nothing without Aslan.

This illustrates a basic biblical principle: we can do nothing without Jesus (Aslan symbolizes Jesus in the world of Narnia). Jesus uses the analogy of a grapevine. He is the Vine, we're the branches, and we can do nothing if we aren't connected to him. Just as a branch can't produce any grapes unless it's connected to the vine, so disciples of Jesus can't produce any fruit unless they stay connected to him. We stay connected to Jesus through prayer and Bible study (John 15:7) and through obedience which comes from our love for him (John 15:10). If we abide in Jesus, stay connected to him, we'll bear fruit (verse 5). That is, we'll be able to do all that God has called us to do (Phil 4:13).

Without Jesus we can do nothing; with him we can do whatever he has called us to do.

---

* Lewis, *The Chronicles of Narnia*, 147.
** Lewis, *The Chronicles of Narnia*, 191.

Today's Reading: 2 Cor 5:18–21

Ambassadors of Christ

THE OXFORD ENGLISH DICTIONARY defines an ambassador as "An official messenger sent by or to a sovereign or public body; *esp.* a minister of high rank sent by one sovereign or state to another."* Paul described himself as an ambassador of Christ (verse 20; Eph 6:20), Christ's representative who made Christ's appeal to the world. Today it's we who are ambassadors of Christ. But what does that mean?

First, Christ's message has been entrusted to us (verse 19). Since Jesus is no longer here in the flesh, it's we who are given the task of preaching the gospel to the world (Matt 28:18–20). We are to call others to become part of the kingdom of God. We may note that just as an ambassador says what their government has instructed them to say, so we must preach Christ's message, not our own. This is part of what it means to live under our King's authority.

Second, being Christ's representatives means that we are called to act in a way that befits a representative of Christ. It has often been said that we're the only Bible some people will ever read. The first sight of our King that unbelievers get is us. We give them their first impression of him. Sadly, the impression that some Christians give of Jesus isn't a good one. Let's be careful to talk and act in a way that makes him look good. This is what Jesus meant when he said, "You are the light of the world . . . Let your light shine before others, that they may see your good deeds and glorify your Father in heaven" (Matt 5:14,16 NIV).

Lord Jesus, I represent you to the world. Help me make you look good.

---

* *Shorter Oxford English Dictionary,* (3rd ed,) s.v. "Ambassador."

Today's Reading: Eph 2:4-9

Rules and Relationship

SEVERAL YEARS AGO I LEARNED a lesson in theology from Scots comic Billy Connolly. Performing live on TV in Scotland, he said, "The church is always saying, 'Thou shalt not.' But this is Scotland, where the men wear skirts, and yes we shall!"[*] In an ironic kind of way, he has a point, because real Christianity isn't about "Thou shalt not."

Genuine, biblical Christianity isn't about rules, it's about having a relationship with God through Jesus. This is a matter which has concerned the church since her beginnings. The first Christians were Jews, brought up to obey the law of Moses. The question is still a crucial one: are we saved by appropriating to ourselves by faith the sacrificial death of Jesus on our behalf, or by earning our way to heaven by keeping rules? The law's standard is absolute perfection, and anyone who breaks even one rule is guilty of having broken them all (Jas 2:10). This standard became a burden which, as Peter himself admits, the Jews were unable to bear (Acts 15:10). That's why Jesus came to earth; he's the only human who has ever been able to meet the law's standard (this is what is meant in Matt 3:15–17; compare Rom 8:3–4). But if we appropriate to ourselves by faith what Jesus has done, we're covered by his perfection and his sacrifice. This is to come into relationship with him. He has done for us what we couldn't do for ourselves. Our part is to believe by faith that "Jesus lived and died for *me*." This is what distinguishes Christianity from other religions. Only Christianity says that we couldn't get up to God, so God came down to us.

Genuine, biblical Christianity isn't about rules, it's about relationship.

---

[*] Smax, *World Tour*, "Episode Six: Edinburgh."

Today's Reading: Gal 6:7–10

As You Sow...

"As you sow, so shall you reap." This saying was first formulated by the Roman politician-writer Cicero (106 BC–43 BC). If a farmer plants wheat seeds, he can expect to harvest wheat; if he plants barley seeds, he can expect to harvest barley. Cicero uses the expression metaphorically—if he criticizes someone, he can expect them to criticize him. Ancient Rome was an agricultural society, so the metaphor was easily understood. Even today, when most of us live in cities, we can understand it.

Paul uses this metaphor in the spiritual sense. His phrasing is a little different from Cicero's, but his meaning is similar. If we sow to the flesh, we'll reap a harvest of corruption; if we sow to the Spirit, we'll reap a harvest of eternal life. Just in case we think we might be able to sow to the flesh and reap eternal life, Paul says, "Do not be deceived: God cannot be mocked" (verse 7 NIV). The law of sowing and reaping, as it's sometimes called, is a principle laid down by God. To think we can be an exception to the rule is to mock God.

What does Paul mean by sowing to the Spirit? It means to live under the Spirit's guidance and control. Paul doesn't say when we'll reap the harvest of sowing to the Spirit; he only says, "in due time." Sometimes we have to do what's right for a long time before we reap the rewards. That's why he encourages his readers not to get weary in doing right (verse 9). But we have God's promise that we'll reap what we sow.

Let's sow to the Spirit rather than the flesh, and not give up, because we'll reap the harvest in due time.

Today's Reading: Prov 18:13; 29:20

A Capital Mistake

AT THE BEGINNING OF Sir Arthur Conan Doyle's "The Adventure of the Second Stain," Sherlock Holmes is preparing to leave his apartment on Baker Street to begin investigating a new case. But he says to Dr. Watson, "I haven't an inkling as to what form [the solution to the mystery] will take. It is a capital mistake to theorize in advance of the facts."* (Similarly in "The Adventure of the Copper Beeches" he exclaims, "Data! Data! Data! . . . I can't make bricks without clay."**) The great detective knows that it's a mistake to jump to conclusions before he knows all the facts of the case.

Jumping to conclusions is as big a mistake for us as it is for Sherlock Holmes. Prov 18:13 NIV says, "To answer before listening—that is folly and shame." And Prov 29:20 NIV says, "Do you see someone who speaks in haste? There is more hope for a fool than for them." Before we draw conclusions or come to an opinion about something, it's best to make sure that we have all the facts. If we don't, it's wisest to reserve judgement. That's not always easy. It takes self-control to refrain from jumping to conclusions, to say, "I don't know."

Along with gathering all the facts, it's also important to check our sources. Are they reliable? This is another part of keeping from jumping to conclusions. It's as well to remember that anyone can say anything they want to on the internet, and there are few restrictions. In this era of misinformation, disinformation, and "fake news," we need to choose wisely whom we trust.

Before we come to a conclusion or form an opinion, let's be careful to gather all the facts and check our sources.

---

* Doyle, *Complete Sherlock Holmes*, 657.
** Doyle, *Complete Sherlock Holmes*, 322.

Suggested Reading: Matt 2:1–12

A Christmas Star

IN DECEMBER 2020 A REGULAR astronomical event occurred which, that year, had a particular significance. There was a conjunction between Jupiter and Saturn. A conjunction happens when two celestial objects appear, from our point of view on Earth, to come close together. In fact, Jupiter and Saturn do this every twenty years. But here's what was unusual about the conjunction of 2020. It's been almost four hundred years since the two planets came as close as they did on December 21, 2020; and it's been eight hundred years since this conjunction happened at night so we could see it. Because this happened so close to Christmas, people called it "the Christmas star." Did God see to it that 2020's conjunction happened at night, at Christmas time? Certainly it was God who set the stars and planets in motion at creation, and he knew from the beginning of time what would happen that year. He knew that at Christmas of 2020 we would need an extra reminder that he is with us.

God has promised that he will never leave us or forsake us (Deut 31:6; Heb 13:5) and that he is with us always (Matt 28:20). In 2020 as much as in any other year, God is with us. This is the meaning of the name Emmanuel, which Isaiah prophesied for Jesus (Isa 7:14; Matt 1:23). Even if we don't feel like he's with us, he's there. We can believe that on the basis of his word. Just as a star pointed the magi to the infant Jesus, so the "Christmas star" of 2020 points us to the God who is with us, even in tough times.

The "Christmas star" of 2020 reminds us that even in turbulent times, God is with us.

Today's Reading: John 11:32–37

Couldn't He...?

I SOMETIMES HEAR FROM PEOPLE who ask questions like, "Why didn't God stop my son from dying?" or, "Why didn't I get the job I wanted?" They're disappointed with God. John 11:32–37 is a passage about disappointment with Jesus. Mary says to him, "If you'd been here, my brother wouldn't have died." There's a certain amount of faith here—she's sure that if he'd been there, he would have done something. But others express disappointment bordering on unbelief: "He healed a blind man, couldn't he have stopped Lazarus from dying?" What they mean is, "Why didn't he stop Lazarus from dying?"

What do we do when God doesn't do what we want, or expect? When he disappoints us? I know what that feels like: my life hasn't turned out the way I thought it would. When that happens, there are a few things that we do well to remember. First, God has a plan for us, and it's a plan for our good, not our harm (Jer 29:11). But he doesn't promise to tell us every detail. Second, God's ways are higher than ours, and his thoughts higher than ours (Isa 55:8–9). We shouldn't expect to understand him. God knows what he's doing, even when we don't know what he's doing. Our part is to trust him. Finally, God isn't obligated to do what we want him to. We must remember that he is sovereign, and let him be in charge in our lives. It isn't easy when God seems to disappoint us. But if we trust him and submit to his authority, he'll work things out for our good.

Father, I don't understand what has happened in my life, and what hasn't happened. But I trust you that your plan for me is good.

Today's Reading: Matt 6:32–33

Cupboard Love

CLEOPATRA ENTWINED HERSELF AROUND my mother's legs, the way cats often do. But my mother wasn't fooled by the display of affection. It was snack time, and my mother was holding a bag of cat treats. "It's just cupboard love," my mother told Cleo. "Cupboard love" is a British expression, which my mother learned from her English grandfather. It means loving someone only for what they can give us or do for us. Sure enough, after my mother had given Cleo her treats, Cleo wandered away.

I wonder how often our love for God is like that. Do we come to him only for what we want him to do for us? It's true that God wants to bless us and meet our needs; we can, and should, go to him for what we need. But if that's the only time we go to him, our relationship with him can become one of you-scratch-my-back-and-I'll-scratch-yours. He is worthy of so much more.

If we put God first, ahead of other things, he'll give us what we need. This is what Jesus meant when he said, "Seek first [God's] kingdom and his righteousness, and all these things will be given to you as well" (Matt 6:33 NIV). I wonder if Jesus' Jewish audience, when they heard this, remembered that centuries earlier God had said, "Man does not live on bread alone but on every word that comes from the mouth of the LORD" (Deut 8:3 NIV). It's a matter of where our priorities are. Let's love God for who he is, not just for what he can do for us. As it's often said, let's seek God's face, not his hand.

Let's seek God for who he is, not just for what he can give us.

Today's Reading: 2 Cor 1:3–4

Comforted to Comfort

I GOT A CALL ON the Prayer Line from a woman who was upset by the noise that the people in the apartment above her made (in fact we regularly get calls on this subject). As I was talking with her, from above me came a house-shaking thumping and banging. The sound of my upstairs neighbor's two children at play (this was also a regular occurrence). It wasn't easy, but God gave me the grace to deal with it. After all, my neighbor couldn't send her kids outside to play in the winter, when it's cold and it gets dark early.

It took a while, but eventually I understood something else. God wanted to use the noise above me to give me empathy for those who were having trouble with noisy, nosy, or otherwise annoying neighbors. Sometimes God's purpose in bringing us through hard times is so that once he has comforted us, we can comfort others in difficulty just as God has comforted us. This is a good thing that God can bring out of a bad situation (see Rom 8:28). This is the recovered alcoholic who counsels those who are trying to get sober, or the divorced woman who ministers to women whose marriages have crumbled. The Christian life is not about us. Sometimes God lets us go through hard things for other people's benefit, so we can minister to them. There's no one who can minister to someone in difficulty like someone who has been there. When we let that happen, we not only serve others but bring God glory.

Father, thank you for the comfort that you've given me through hard times. Help me be as much of a comfort to others as you've been to me.

Today's Reading: Eph 4:26–27

Danger, Anger

ONE OF COMICDOM'S MOST iconic characters is the Hulk. The Hulk is a large green monster who goes on destructive rampages. But he is also Bruce Banner, an atomic scientist who was exposed to gamma rays. Since that accident, when Banner gets angry or stressed, he turns into the Hulk. It's easy to see why this character is so iconic. Few of us have "hulked out" and gone on an angry, destructive rampage. But most of us have, at some point, said or done something in anger which they later regretted (I know I have). "Anger is cruel and fury overwhelming" (Prov 27:4 NIV).

It's not surprising, then, that the Bible warns about the danger of anger. Paul wrote that even when we're angry we shouldn't sin by letting the sun go down with us still angry, because if we do, we give the devil a foothold in our lives (Eph 4:26–28). And James wrote, "Everyone should be quick to listen, slow to speak and slow to become angry, because human anger does not produce the righteousness that God desires" (Jas 1:19–20 NIV). So it's important that we deal with anger as soon as we feel it. We do this by giving our feelings to God. Since our anger is often caused by our being hurt, let's give our hurt to God and trust him to deal with it. Our heavenly Father doesn't take it lightly when his children get hurt. He will deal with hurtful situations if we let him deal with them rather than taking things into our own hands. Let's trust God enough to let him heal our hurts.

Better a patient person than a warrior, one with self-control than one who takes a city. (Prov 16:32 NIV).

Today's Reading: Rev 21:1–5

Our Ultimate Hope

It's the end of January, and after what seems like weeks of cloudiness, and a snowfall that was epic even by Ontario standards, the sun is shining. Yesterday evening, I didn't have to close my window blinds until almost 6:00. The days are getting longer. It's still cold, but there are hints that winter is beginning to release its icy grip. In the news, there are signs that COVID-19 is beginning to release its grip on us. Spring is coming. In spring the earth is renewed. Winter's brownish grass turns green, the trees get leaves and plants begin to come up. The temperature rises and so do our hopes.

The Bible offers us hope of a renewal even greater than the renewal of spring. If anyone is in Christ, that person is a new creation (2 Cor 5:17). We can walk in newness of life now (Rom 6:4). We can have the abundant life that Jesus came to give us (John 10:10). But there's more. The raising of Lazarus (John 11:1–44) and the resurrection of Jesus himself are only a foretaste of what is to come for us. "For if we have been united with him in a death like his, we will certainly also be united with him in a resurrection like his" (Rom 6:5 NIV). And it won't be just we that get renewed: one day God will make all things new (Rev 21:5). As renewed people we'll live in a new heaven and a new earth (Rev 21:1–4). This is our greatest hope, the hope of the ultimate renewal. Until then, creation itself reminds us that the ultimate renewal is coming.

Father, as the earth is renewed in spring, we look to you for renewal, both now and forever. Amen.

Today's Reading: 1 Thess 5:16–18

Thankful in All Circumstances

It hasn't been an easy two years for me. During that time I moved house three times in less than three months, and then again several months later. In May 2021 my mother passed away after a short illness. I've had financial struggles. And in the background the entire time has been the pandemic which has made things so difficult for everyone. Yet in all this I'm thankful for God's provision and care. He knows what's happening, and he's got this.

The apostle Paul wrote to the church in Thessalonica, "Give thanks in all circumstances" (1 Thess. 5:18 NIV). So how do we do that? We may notice that Paul says to give thanks *in* all circumstances, not *for* all circumstances. But what does that mean? To give thanks in all circumstances means to be thankful that God is in charge in every situation, and that he knows what he's doing, even when we don't know what he's doing. There's a strong element in this of trust in God's sovereignty, goodness, and love. Trusting like that isn't always easy. But God will do what he knows is right and best, even if it doesn't seem like that to our limited understanding. "In all things God works for the good of those who love him, who have been called according to his purpose." (Rom. 8:28 NIV). This doesn't mean that all things *are* good, but that God brings good things out of bad circumstances. God is good, and he loves us, and he can be trusted. He is always in control. That's why we can be thankful in all circumstances.

Thank you Father that you are in charge in every situation. I trust you to bring good things out of my bad circumstances.

Today's Reading: Jas 1:5

Every Great Decision...

I'M A FAN OF THE long-running British science-fiction TV series *Doctor Who*. In the 1988 story "Remembrance of the Daleks" the Doctor says, "Every great decision creates ripples, like a huge boulder dropped in a lake. The ripples merge, rebound off the banks in unforeseeable ways. The heavier the decision, the larger the waves, and the more uncertain the consequences." In the context, the Doctor is beginning to realize that an action that he took several lifetimes previously is having consequences that he didn't foresee. He has made a grave error of judgment.*

That great decisions have great consequences is as true for humans as it is for Time Lords. And I know the paralysis that can come from dwelling too much on "What will happen if I do this, or that?" So what's a mere human to do? How can we avoid what has been called "the paralysis of analysis"? Believers have a way of avoiding that trap. Jas 1:5 says that we can ask God for wisdom when we need it, and he'll give us all the wisdom we need, and he won't criticise us for asking. And Prov 3:5-6 says, "Trust in the LORD with all your heart and lean not on your own understanding; in all your ways submit to him, and he will make your paths straight" (NIV).

Our understanding is often incomplete, but God's understanding is not. That means that there will be things that we can't foresee, but God knows about them in advance. If we ask God for wisdom as we make decisions, he'll give us the guidance we need to make right choices. Then we can trust him to work out the consequences.

If we ask God for wisdom, he'll help us make wise decisions.

---

* Morgan, *Doctor Who*, "Remembrance."

Today's Reading: Eph 6:10–17

A Defeated Foe

"The enemy is having a heyday with me." "The devil is really attacking me." We hear statements like this frequently at the ministry. And there's truth in them. We do have an enemy, the devil, and he will attack us if we give we give him the opportunity. But that's not the whole story.

Some Christians are surprised when the enemy attacks them. But Jesus never promised us a trouble-free life. In fact, he said, "In the world you will have trouble." But he then said, "Take heart! I have overcome the world" (John 16:33 NIV). By his death and resurrection Jesus has done everything that needed to be done to defeat Satan. We'll have some battles to fight, but Jesus has already won the war. It's tempting to wish that the enemy would just leave us alone. But as long as we're in this world and on God's side, that's not going to happen. But we don't have to just put up with it.

When the enemy attacks us, we can fight back. Jesus has given us authority over the devil (Luke 10:19) and weapons that will be effective against him (Eph 6:13–17). Prayer is also a weapon (Eph 6:18–20). And if we think, speak, and act the way God wants us to, we'll avoid giving the enemy a foothold in our lives (Eph 4:25–27). And God's presence and protection are with us as well (Ps 91). So we don't have to be afraid of the enemy, because God has given us everything we need to deal with him. We just need to make use of what God has given us.

The devil is a defeated foe. We'll have some battles to fight, but Jesus has already won the war.

Today's Reading: Rom 5:3–5

When the Pressure is On

I RECENTLY LEARNED A LESSON in geology: diamonds aren't made from coal. Coal is a sedimentary rock formed from long-dead plants, no deeper than two miles below the earth's surface. But diamonds are formed in certain places in the earth's mantle, 90 miles (150 km.) or more beneath the surface. Here the temperature is an unimaginable 2000 degrees Fahrenheit (1050 C) or hotter. But there's more. These diamond-producing areas, known as "diamond stability zones," are usually found in the centers of continental plates, with the weight of an entire continent pressing down on them. Only in these extreme conditions do the carbon atoms that make up the diamonds form the cubic lattice structure that gives diamonds their strength.* Anything less produces graphite, with its weak single-layer lattice structure.

God does the same in our lives. This is what Paul means in Rom. 5:3–5: suffering produces perseverance, perseverance produces Christian character, and Christian character produces a hope that doesn't disappoint us, because it's powered by God's love. The Holy Spirit operating in our hearts (which begins when we're born again) assures us that God loves us. Knowing that God loves us gives us a hope that doesn't disappoint us by breaking down under the heat and pressure of difficult times. Similarly James challenges his readers to see trials as opportunities for spiritual growth, because trials that test our faith in God give us endurance. And if we let endurance do all that God intends it to do, we'll become spiritually mature (Jas 1:2–4). Then we can be all God that wants us to be, and be strong enough to do all that he wants us to do.

When the pressure is on, God is making us into diamonds for his use and his glory.

---

* This information from King, "Diamonds."

Today's Reading: Phil 3:12–14

Don't Look Back

A STAPLE OF OLD MOVIES is a scene in which the hero and heroine climb a steep cliff or the outside of a tall structure. Inevitably the hero says to the heroine, "Don't look down!" If they look down, they'll fall to their deaths. The only way to safety is upwards. God's word to us is not "Don't look down," but "Don't look back!"

Some Christians are trapped in their sinful past. They're so focused on what they did, sometimes years previously, that they can't let it go and move on. They can't stop remembering the past. But God says, "I, I am He who blots out your transgressions for my own sake, and I will not remember your sins" (Isa 43:25 RSV). The phrasing "I will not remember" suggests not that God has suffered a lapse of memory, but rather that he has chosen not to remember our sins. And if he doesn't remember our sins, then there's no need for us to remember them either. Similarly Micah 7:19 says, "You [God] will again have compassion on us; you will tread our sins underfoot and hurl all our iniquities into the depths of the sea" (NIV). But how can this be? How can God forgive and forget like this? It's all because of what Jesus did on the cross. His death has paid the price for our sins. So God is both just in demanding a payment for sin and faithful in keeping his promise to forgive (1 John 1:9). All this means that we don't have to be stuck in a past that God has forgiven and forgotten. We can live in the forgiveness that Jesus died for us to have.

Let's not keep remembering what God has forgiven and forgotten.

Today's Reading: 2 Tim 1:6–8

Fighting Fear

FEAR CAN CRIPPLE US. It can keep us from fulfilling God's call on our lives. And there's a lot of it out there right now. COVID-19 has caused a pandemic of fear, and brought out other fears that were less visible. But when fear comes against us, we can fight back, and the Bible tells us how.

Fear doesn't come from God. In 2 Tim 1:7 Paul tells Timothy, "God did not give us a spirit of timidity but a spirit of power and love and self-control" (RSV). In the context, Paul is encouraging Timothy not to allow fear to stop him from doing what God has called him to do. With the phrase, "by the power of God" (verse 8 NIV) Paul reminds Timothy that God hasn't called Timothy to do something only to leave him high and dry, without the strength to do it. And God won't do that to us either. Phil 4:13 says that we can do all things through the one who strengthens us. The Bible gives us only one reason why we shouldn't be afraid, and that is that God is with us. Ps 23:4 says, "I will fear no evil, for you are with me" (NIV). And Josh 1:9 says, "Do not be afraid . . . for the Lord your God will be with you wherever you go" (NIV).

All this doesn't mean that we'll never feel fear, or that fearful things will never happen to us. God doesn't promise that. It does mean that we don't have to be paralysed by fear, because God promises that when fearful things do happen, he'll be with us and bring us through.

When fear comes against us, we can fight back. We don't need to be afraid, because God is with us.

Today's Reading: Isa 43:2–4

Flowers in the Dark

MANY YEARS AGO I WAS BLESSED to be able to spend some time in Honolulu, Hawaii. There I saw a flower that blooms only at night. This was the night-blooming cereus, which opens to show its beauty and spread its fragrance only in the dark (at that time there were no night-blooming plants in Canada). But why would God create flowers that show themselves only at night?

For me, the night-blooming flowers remind us that God is with us in the dark and difficult times. A particularly well-known Scripture on this is Ps 23:4, "Even though I walk through the darkest valley, I will fear no evil, for you are with me" (NIV). And in Job 35:10, Elihu describes God as the one "who gives songs in the night" (RSV). Another very well-known verse is Isa 43:2: "When you pass through the waters I will be with you; and through the rivers, they shall not overwhelm you; when you walk through fire you shall not be burned, and the flame shall not consume you" (RSV). We may notice that this verse says "when," not "if." God never promises us that we'll never have dark times; he does promise that he will be with us and bring us through the dark times, because he loves us (Isa 43:4). Some Christians think that if they go through difficult times, it means that God doesn't love them. But that's a lie that the enemy uses to discourage us. When we go through dark times, that's the time to look beyond our circumstances and our emotions, and trust in God's promise that he is with us (Matt 28:20; Heb 13:5).

The night-blooming flowers remind us that God is with us in the dark and difficult times.

Today's Reading: Eph 1:4–14

The Cure for Insecurity

PEOPLE OFTEN CALL THE PRAYER LINE for prayer about their insecurity. Insecurity is a major weapon that the enemy uses to keep Christians from being effective against him and for God. I know of only one way to fight insecurity: to know who we are in Christ. To see ourselves the way God sees us.

It isn't always easy to believe what God says about us, especially when we're hearing otherwise from family, bosses, or co-workers. But God's opinion of us is the one that matters. What he says about us trumps whatever anyone else might say.

Here's a small sample of what God says about us:

- If we're in Christ, we're a new creation (2 Cor 5:17).
- We're the righteousness of God in Christ (2Cor 5:21).
- God will strengthen us to do whatever he wants us to do (Phil 4:13).
- We're dead to sin and alive to God, we don't need to be controlled by sin (Rom 6:6–7).
- We're part of God's family, his adopted children (Eph 2:19; 1:5).
- We're members of the body of Christ (1 Cor 12:27)
- We're complete in Christ (Col 2:10).
- We're hidden with Christ in God, under his protection (Col 3:3).

And so much more!

All these good things are only true about us because we're in Christ. They're true because of him, not because of us. And it can take time before they're apparent in our lives. But they're still true. When we know who we are in Christ, we can face the world with confidence, because the real source of our confidence is Christ, not ourselves. We are loved, forgiven, and able to do whatever God has called us to do.

The cure for insecurity is knowing who we are in Christ.

Today's Reading: Eph 2:8–10

The Master Artist

I AM CRAFTING YOU. The thought came to me out of the blue, so strongly that I knew for sure that it was a word from God. And I knew what it meant, because I'm into crafts. I knit, crochet and do embroidery. I make my stitcheries carefully and patiently, using the colours and patterns that I choose. By the time I finish a piece of work, it looks exactly the way I want it to.

God is also at work in our lives. Stitch by stitch he makes us into the men and women he wants us to be. A Scripture that has long been important to me is Phil 1:6: "He who began a good work in you will bring it to completion at the day of Christ (RSV)." God is at work in each of our lives, building Christian character in us and developing in us the skills and characteristics we need in order to do what he has called us to do. This is also what Paul means in Eph 2:10. None of us will look like any of our brothers and sisters in Christ, because God's call on each of our lives is unique.

I took God's word to me as an assurance that he was at work in me, making me into the woman that he wants me to be. The Master Artist uses the dark times, and the bright ones, to fashion us as he chooses. Being crafted isn't always easy or pleasant, but it turns us into something beautiful—God's own handmade, one-of-a-kind masterpiece, perfectly suited for what he wants to do through us.

God is making us into what he wants us to be, so we can do what he wants us to do.

Today's Reading: 1 Tim 6:6–10

American Dream?

ANYONE CAN GET RICH if they work hard enough. And if they get rich enough, they can buy power, material goods, and status in society. This is what is known as the American Dream (though it's not only Americans who believe in it). But what does the Bible have to say about money and material goods?

In 1 Tim 6:6–10, Paul gives two reasons why Christians should be content with what they have. The first reason is that "you can't take it with you." So we should be content if we have food and clothing. The other reason to be content with what we have is that desire for wealth opens the door to sin. It's a trap that leads to painful consequences. We may note that verse 10 is often misquoted: it isn't money itself that is the root of all kinds of evil, but our attitude toward it, the love of money. If we honor God with our finances by putting God ahead of money, he'll meet our needs. He'll provide for us so that we have food, clothing, and shelter. The way we show that we honor God in this area is to pay our tithes and to be as generous as we can with what we have. "God is able to provide you with every blessing in abundance, so that you may always have enough of everything and may provide in abundance for every good work" (2 Cor 9:8 RSV). In fact, this is the only area in which God challenges us to test him and see if he'll keep his promise (Mal 3:10). Let's keep money in its place.

Father, help me keep a proper perspective on money and material goods. I trust you to meet my needs.

Today's Reading: Heb 4:14–16

Humble Enough to Dare

THE HORSE AND HIS BOY is the third book in C.S. Lewis's *Chronicles of Narnia* series. The horse of the title is Bree, a Narnian Talking Horse who has spent most of his life in servitude in the land of Calormen. Bree has decided to escape and return to Narnia. But he soon loses his eagerness to get to Narnia. He has become self-conscious and wants to look better before he enters Narnia. Then Aslan the great Lion (who symbolizes Jesus in Narnia) appears to Bree, saying, "You poor, proud frightened Horse, draw near. Nearer still, my son. Do not dare not to dare."*

I have talked with many people whose problem is the same as Bree's. They want to come to church and become Christians, but feel that the need to clean themselves up first. But this gets things in the wrong order. We come to God first, and he cleans us up. The truth is that we can't clean ourselves up. To think that we can is pride. We don't need to hesitate to ask God to clean us up. "If we confess our sins, [God] is faithful and just, and will forgive our sins and cleanse us from all unrighteousness" (1 John 1:9 RSV). We can dare to come to God as we are. We don't dare not to dare, because we can't cleanse ourselves from sin. That's why Jesus came and paid the price for our sins on the cross. Because the price has been paid, God will cleanse us from sin if we repent and ask him to forgive us. Let's dare to be humble enough to come to God as we are.

We come to God as we are, and he cleans us up.

---

* Lewis, *The Chronicles of Narnia*, 299.

Today's Reading: Ps 89:6

One-of-a-Kind

CRAFT SHOWS OFTEN ADVERTISE that their wares are one-of-a-kind. We value something unique more highly than something mass-produced. Its uniqueness makes it precious.

God is also one-of-a-kind. Let's consider some ways in which God is unique.

- God is unique in holiness. "Who among the gods is like you, LORD? Who is like you—majestic in holiness, awesome in glory, working wonders?" (Exod 15:11 NIV).
- Because God is holy, he is also just. "The LORD is known by his acts of justice; the wicked are ensnared by the work of their hands" (Ps 9:16 NIV).
- God is just, but he is also merciful. "Who is a God like you, who pardons sin and forgives the transgression of the remnant of his inheritance? You do not stay angry forever, but delight to show mercy" (Mic 7:18 NIV).
- This combination of justice and mercy is also unique. Some humans are just, and some are merciful; but which humans are both just and merciful? That's why the psalmist exclaims, "Love and faithfulness meet together; righteousness and peace kiss each other" (Ps 85:10 NIV). The ultimate meeting of God's justice and God's mercy is in Jesus.
- God's love is unique, because he loves those who don't deserve it. "God shows his love for us in that while we were yet sinners Christ died for us" (Rom 5:8 RSV).
- God is unique in power. "There is none like thee, O LORD; thou art great, and thy name is great in might. Who would not fear thee, O King of the nations? For this is thy due; for . . . in all their kingdoms there is none like thee" (Jer 10:6–7 RSV).

"How great you are, Sovereign LORD! There is no one like you, and there is no God but you." (2 Sam 7:22 NIV).

Today's Reading: Mark 9:2–3, 9, 14–15

Back to Real Life

IT HAD BEEN A GREAT CONFERENCE, a real mountaintop experience. But now everyone had to go home. Andrea wondered how she could take the experience with her. How could it be of use to her in real life, with her real circumstances?

When Jesus, Peter, James, and John came down from the mountain after Jesus' transfiguration, a crowd was waiting for them. The disciples had had an extraordinary experience. They'd seen Jesus as they'd never seen him before. But now they had come down, and there was work to do. They had to take what they had learned with them, and use in the valley what they had seen on the mountaintop.

How do we take a mountaintop experience back to real life? God wants us to take what we learn on the mountaintop back into the humdrum of everyday life, and apply it there. It will help to take plenty of notes, and to study them after we get home. That will help us remember what we learned. We should also understand that when we get home, there will still be our spouses, children, and homes to take care of. We'll still have the same job to go back to, and the same co-workers will still be there. Our circumstances will be the same—but we don't need to be the same. We can allow God to use mountaintop experiences to change us. To equip us to deal with our circumstances in a godly way. God is with us in real life, in our real circumstances and our real problems.

Father, help me take what you teach me on the mountaintop and use it in real life. This is one way that you equip me to deal with my real-life circumstances.

Today's Reading: Rom 12:18–21

Leave Room for Wrath

THE TV SERIES *PERSON OF INTEREST* is about a team of people who anticipate crimes. Their supercomputer gives them the Social Security Numbers of people who are about to be involved in a crime, whether as victim or perpetrator. If the number turns out to be a perpetrator, the team's job is to prevent the number from committing the crime. In these episodes, the perpetrator often wants to get revenge on someone who has hurt them. So the team tries to persuade them that there's a better way than vengeance.

That got me thinking—what does the Bible say about getting revenge? What does God want us to do when we've been hurt? The apostle Paul deals with this in Rom 12:18–20. He says two things, and neither of them makes sense from a human point of view. First he says, "Leave room for God's wrath" (Rom 12:19 NIV). But what does that mean? It means to put the situation into God's hands and let him deal with it. This is contrary to our human inclinations. It isn't easy. But our heavenly Father doesn't take it lightly when someone hurts one of his children. If we let him, he'll deal with it. But taking things into our own hands blocks God from intervening in the situation.

Then Paul goes even further: if we see our enemy in need, we should help (verse 20). This is likely to be the opposite of what we want to do. But such kindness can lead the offender to repent (verse 20; compare Rom 2:4). This is what Jesus meant when he told us to love our enemies and do good to them (Luke 6:27–28). This is dealing with hurt God's way.

Getting revenge is God's department, not ours.

Today's Reading: Rom 5:6–8

The Sacrifice

THE BBC-TV SERIES *FATHER BROWN* is based on G. K. Chesterton's priest-detective. It is set in the 1950s. In the Season 3 episode "The Standing Stones," polio is rampaging through the village of Standing. Many children have become ill, and several have died. In desperation, the villagers have turned to pagan ways, and decided to offer a human sacrifice. An innocent life will be offered to prevent the loss of more innocent lives. The first attempted sacrifice fails; but as the pagans are about to offer up one of their own, Father Brown willingly takes the man's place.*

Jesus offered himself as a sacrifice for us, to save us from the spiritual death which was the penalty for our sin. He could take our place because he was innocent, without sin. Jesus took on our sin and gave us his righteousness. As Peter puts it, "Christ also died for sins once for all, the righteous for the unrighteous, that he might bring us to God" (1 Pet 3:18 RSV). And as Paul puts it, "For our sake [God] made him to be sin who knew no sin, so that in him we might become the righteousness of God" (2 Cor 5:21 RSV). This is what is sometimes called the Great Exchange. Jesus didn't wait to sacrifice himself for us until we became righteous or until we deserved it; he sacrificed himself for us while we were sinners (Rom 5:8). The death of the Substitute on our behalf has been accepted. Because the sinless Jesus died in our place, we can have eternal life. All we have to do is appropriate this death to ourselves by believing that "Jesus died for me."

The sacrificial death of Jesus means eternal life for us.

---

* Carter, *Father Brown*, "Standing Stones."

Today's Reading: Eph 2:8–9

"Salvation Panic"

C.J. Sansom's Matthew Shardlake mysteries feature a lawyer living in London at the end of the reign of King Henry VIII. In *Revelation* Shardlake meets Adam Kite, a teenager who suffers from what was then called "salvation panic." Adam believes that God won't forgive his sins, that he doesn't deserve to be saved and will spend eternity in hell.* There are a lot of people today who suffer from "salvation panic," and it's based on a lie from the enemy.

There are two lies at the root of "salvation panic." The first lie is that our sin could be too big for God to forgive. But that's not true. There's nothing that God will not forgive those who genuinely repent (1 John 1:9). The second lie is that God won't forgive us unless we deserve it. But God doesn't forgive us because we deserve it. He forgives us because of what Jesus did on the cross. All we have to do is to believe that what Jesus did, he did *for us*. To accept his offer of salvation. Deserving has nothing to do with it. To be saved because we deserve it would be salvation by works. But what God offers us is salvation by faith, through his grace (Eph 2:8–9). This is based on God's love for us—God loves us because of who he is, not who we are. So we don't need to strive to earn our salvation. Everything that needs to be done for our salvation has already been done at Calvary. All we need to do is to believe that.

There's nothing that God will not forgive those who genuinely repent. He forgives us not because we deserve it but because of what Jesus did on the cross.

---

* Sansom, *Revelation*, 18–19.

Today's Reading: Phil 2:14–15

Shine Like Stars

ON A DARK NIGHT you can't miss the stars; their brightness makes them stand out against the night sky. This is the analogy that Paul uses in Phil 2:14–15. Just as the brightness of stars contrasts with the darkness of the night sky, Christians should stand out against the darkness of the world around them. Paul mentions three ways by which Christians can shine like stars: by submitting to God's will for our lives; by being "blameless and innocent" (verse 15 RSV) in the eyes of the world; and by being "without blemish" (verse 15 RSV) before God.*

Let's look at these three ways to shine and stand out. First, we submit to what God is doing in our lives. This is what it means to "do everything without grumbling or arguing" (verse 14 NIV). Grumbling and arguing with God instead of obeying him shows both a lack of respect for his authority and a lack of trust in his love and goodness. Second, to shine like stars we need to be blameless before the world. To be people of honesty and integrity in a world where compromise is condoned and wrong is rampant. We are to point people to God by showing them that there's a better way to live than the world's way. That isn't always easy. But the Holy Spirit within us will help us. Third, to shine like stars we need to be blameless before God, living uprightly and obediently the way he wants us to. That's how we shine brightly in a dark world.

"You are the light of the world. . . Let your light shine before others, that they may see your good deeds and glorify your Father in heaven" (Matt 5:14, 16 NIV).

---

* Boice, *Philippians*, 169–72.

Today's Reading: Lam 3:18, 21–24

Snow in April

It's not unknown to have snow flurries in Toronto at the beginning of April. But by the end of April the hope of spring is in the air. Nonetheless, one morning near the end of last April I woke up to find a thick blanket of wet, heavy snow in my back yard. And the wind had blocked the narrow walkway which was the only exit from my apartment with a 1m/3' high snowdrift. I'm not a fan of snow even in winter, so I was not impressed. So much for the hope of spring!

Jeremiah, who wrote the book of Lamentations, knew what it was like to have his hopes dashed. That Gentiles should conquer Israel was something that neither Jeremiah nor any other Israelite would have expected. "My splendor is gone, and all that I had hoped from the LORD," (Lam 3:18 NIV) he says. But he also knew that God's love and faithfulness don't change with our circumstances. Choosing to remember that ("call to mind," verse 21) gave Jeremiah hope in the midst of tragedy.

Unexpected and unpleasant things happen, it's part of life in this world. But God is still good. His love and faithfulness don't mean that he'll always do what we want or expect him to do, or what feels pleasant to us. But he'll do what is right and what is best. God is sovereign, and he knows what he's doing, even when we don't know what he's doing. When bad things happen and we don't understand, that's when we need to trust God. Trust in his sovereignty, love, faithfulness, and goodness.

God's love and faithfulness don't mean that he'll always do what we want or expect him to do, or what feels pleasant to us.

Today's Reading: Matt 22:34–40

Summing Up

MIKE CAME OUT OF the training session with his head spinning. His supervisor had thrown a lot of information at him, very quickly! In the lunchroom he shared this with Steve, an older and more experienced colleague. Steve said, "I took the same session a few years ago, I know what you mean. But I can sum it up for you." Steve was able to sum the session up into a few principles that Mike could easily remember.

I wonder if Jews of Jesus' day felt the way Mike did. By this time, the teachers of the law had multiplied the Ten Commandments into 613! How could an average Jew even remember them all, let alone keep them? Maybe this is what Jesus meant when he scolded the teachers of the law for loading the people with heavy burdens and doing nothing to help them bear them (Luke 11:46). Jesus summed up the teachings of the law and the prophets in two principles: to love the Lord with all none's heart, soul, and mind (verse 37) and to love one's neighbor as oneself (verse 37). That's why Paul wrote that anyone who loves their neighbor has fulfilled the law (Rom 13:8–9). If we love God, we won't break any of the first five commandments. If we love our neighbor, we won't steal from them, jealously want what is theirs, or break any other of the last five commandments. These two principles are easy to remember, even if they aren't always easy to live out. But God through the Holy Spirit will help us love the way we should.

Father, it's not always easy to love the way I should. Help me love you with all my being, and love my neighbor as myself.

Today's Reading: Ps 33:20–22

Soon

WHEN I WAS A TEENAGER I babysat a two-year-old boy. It wouldn't be too long after his parents left before he would ask anxiously, "Mommy's coming back?" I would reassure him, "Yes, Mommy's coming back soon." But a short time later he would ask again if his mother was coming back, and I'd reassure him again. To him, "soon" meant "in two minutes."

I wonder if we do something similar when we're waiting on God. We expect God to act immediately, and become angry or resentful if he doesn't. Most of us aren't very good at waiting on God. But God doesn't work on our schedule.

It's kind of a cliché to say that God's timing isn't our timing. But these things become clichés because there's truth in them. So if God's timing isn't our timing, how do we wait on God? Waiting on God requires us to be quiet and listen for his guidance. It requires submission and trust. This is what it means to be still and know that he is God (Ps 46:10). This is something I must admit I'm not good at! It isn't easy, because we want to be in control of our lives, including knowing when things will happen. Waiting on God requires spending time in his written word. If God doesn't act when we want him to, sometimes that's because he's preparing things that we don't know about, making the path ahead of us straight where we can't see it. Sometimes it's us that he's preparing, because the reason for the delay is that we aren't as ready for what we want as we think we are.

God's timing may not be our timing, but it's always the right timing. Let's trust him enough to wait on him.

Today's Reading: Ps 17:1–2, 8–12, 15

God Our Vindicator

IN SIR ARTHUR CONAN DOYLE'S "The Adventure of the Norwood Builder" (first published 1903) John Hector McFarlane asks Sherlock Holmes for help because he has been accused of murder. When Holmes talks with McFarlane's mother, she says, "There is a God in heaven, Mr. Holmes, and that same God . . . will show, in His own good time, that my son's hands are guiltless of [the murdered man's] blood."* She is relying on God to be her son's Vindicator.

In Ps 17, David found himself in a situation similar to McFarlane's. David was surrounded by enemies; verses 9–12 may indicate that he had been falsely accused of something. But he insists that he is innocent (verses 1–5). And he knows that God knows that he is innocent (verse 3). So he doesn't hesitate to call on God for help (verses 6–8). David also knows that God knows what David's accusers have been saying; and he knows that God is just. So he doesn't hesitate to ask God to deal with the accusers (verses 13–14). The psalm ends with a final expression of confidence that God will vindicate David (verse 15). This is, in part, what Jesus meant in the parable of the Widow and the Unjust Judge (Luke 18:1–8). If a judge who is not only human but corrupt will give justice, "will not God vindicate his elect, who cry to him day and night? Will he delay long over them? I tell you, he will vindicate them speedily" (verses 7–8 RSV).

Maybe you've been accused of something you didn't do, or you've been denied justice. God knows the truth, nothing is hidden from him. God your Vindicator will bring the truth out.

We can trust God to be our Vindicator.

---

* Doyle, *Complete Sherlock Holmes*, 503

Today's Reading: Ps 55:12–19

Our Unchanging God

It has been a time of change for me. My mother moved into a seniors' facility, so after many years of living with her, I've moved into my own apartment. But between "there" and "here" there have been two other moves. Maybe you've also experienced changes, whether good or bad, this year, in your job or in your family life. And I write this at the end of 2020, a year in which so much has changed for everyone.

But there's one thing, or rather one person, that hasn't changed—God hasn't changed. Our circumstances may change, but God doesn't. Heb 13:8 says, "Jesus Christ is the same yesterday, today, and forever" (NIV). From the context (verses 7–8) we can see that writer means that the Jesus in whom the church leaders have placed their faith is the same Jesus in whom the readers have placed their faith.

In Ps 55:12–19, David laments that a close friend has turned against him. But he knows that God, who hasn't changed, will rescue him. He knows that God's love for him hasn't changed, and that God's character hasn't changed. This is what Ps 136 means with its repeated refrain, "His love endures forever" (NIV). The Hebrew word translated "love" (other translations have "mercy" or "lovingkindness") is *chesed*. This is covenant love, love backed by commitment.

The God whom David and the Israelites could count on then is the same God whom we can count on now. His character hasn't changed, and his love for his people hasn't changed. God is the one person we can count on not to change. In the changing seasons of our lives, in a rapidly changing world, God is our unmoving Anchor.

Our circumstances may change, but our God doesn't.

Today's Reading: Num 23:19

Truth

ONE OF MY FAVOURITE STORIES in the long-running British science-fiction TV series *Doctor Who* is the 1976 story "The Deadly Assassin." Near the end of this story the Doctor repeats something that his teacher, Borusa, used to say: "Only in mathematics will we find truth." In the context, the Doctor is noting with irony that Borusa (now a high-ranking politician) wants to manipulate the truth to cover up a political scandal.*

There is a truth in mathematics. Two plus two will always equal four; this principle of repeatability is foundational to science. But there's a truth that goes deeper than mathematics, or any other science (though science doesn't contradict it). That truth is the truth of God's word, both written and spoken.

Both Old and New Testaments attest to this. Isa 45:19 says, "I the LORD speak the truth, I declare what is right" (RSV). And a well-known verse on this subject is Num 23:19: "God is not human, that he should lie, not a human being, that he should change his mind. Does he speak and then not act? Does he promise and not fulfill?" (NIV). Similarly in Isa 46:10 God says, "I make known the end from the beginning, from ancient times, what is still to come. I say, 'My purpose will stand, and I will do all that I please.'" (NIV). In the New Testament, Jesus said that God's word is truth (John 17:17). So perhaps it's not surprising that Jesus said that he, the Word made flesh (John 1:14), is the truth (John 14:6). God's word is a reliable guide for our lives. This is why God's word is a lamp for our feet and a light for our path (Ps 119:105).

God's word is trustworthy and truthful.

---

* Maloney, *Doctor Who*, "The Deadly Assassin."

Today's Reading: 1 Pet 3:3–4

Real Beauty

THE COSMETICS INDUSTRY IS WORTH billions of dollars every year. Women especially are spending a lot of money to make themselves look good. And then there's the time and effort we spend on our appearance. Women who don't conform to the world's standard of beauty can feel at a disadvantage. And losing our beauty to age or illness can be very painful. This was as true in Peter's day as it is in ours. Women went in for ornate up-dos and hair ornaments, accompanied by much gold jewelry and elegant dresses. The Bible, however, speaks of a different standard of beauty.

For Christian women, real beauty doesn't come from a cosmetics jar or a clothing store. Rather it comes from "the unfading beauty of a gentle and quiet spirit, which is of great worth in God's sight" (verse 4 NIV). The Greek word translated "gentle" is *praus*, which refers to being humble or considerate (the noun form of this word is listed among the fruit of the Spirit; Gal 5:22). The Greek word translated "quiet" is *hēsuchios*; this means a spirit at rest, a spirit that doesn't allow itself to be troubled by the ups and downs of everyday life. This kind of restraint and stability aren't always easy to maintain; maybe that's why God values them so highly. This inward beauty is "unfading" (NIV; RSV "imperishable") and doesn't wear out or diminish with age. This may be another reason why it's so valuable. This is beauty that lasts, because it's spiritual, not physical. In a world where external beauty seems to be all that matters, let's focus on the beauty that really matters.

Real beauty doesn't come from a cosmetics jar or a clothing store, but from a gentle and quiet spirit.

Today's Reading: Ps 91:14–16

You Can Call Anytime

SOMETIMES PEOPLE CALL THE PRAYER LINE and say that they've had trouble getting through to us. This is regrettable. But we take almost fifteen hundred calls every twenty-four hours, and we've taken calls from every continent on earth (except maybe Antarctica). We do our best to take every call that comes in, but we aren't always able to.

The good news is, God is able to do better than we are. We can get through to him anytime. We'll never get a busy signal or an answering machine. "The eyes of the LORD are on the righteous, and his ears are attentive to their cry" (Ps 34:15 NIV). That's why David could say, "I call out to the LORD, and he answers me from his holy mountain" (Ps 3:4 NIV). And again, "I call on you, my God, for you will answer me; turn your ear to me and hear my prayer" (Ps 17:6 NIV).

Someone once asked me, "How can God hear everyone who's praying to him, all at the same time?" I answered, "Because he's God. We can't do it, but he can." God isn't human, so he doesn't have human limitations. So we can call out to him in prayer anytime, day or night, and be confident that he'll hear us. That doesn't mean that God will do what we want him to do, when we want him to do it. But he always hears our prayers. God says to those who love him, "When they call to me, I will answer them; I will be with them in trouble, I will rescue them and honor them" (Ps 91:15 NRSV).

Thank you Father that I can call on you anytime, knowing that you'll hear me. I can always get through to you.

Today's Reading: 1 Cor 1:10–13

Not Distracted

THE 1981 MOVIE *CHARIOTS OF FIRE* contrasts the lives of two Olympic runners, Harold Abrahams and Eric Liddell. The first time they race against each other, Abrahams comes second to Liddell because he looks to see where Liddell is.* To win the race, a runner must stay focused on their own lane, and not allow themselves to be distracted by looking at the other runners.

This is also true of the Christian life. Competition was a problem in the church in Corinth. After only a few years in existence, the Corinthian church had become divided into several factions. Paul reminds them of where their focus should be: "Is Christ divided? Was Paul crucified for you? Were you baptized in the name of Paul?" (1 Cor 1:13). Similarly the writer of Hebrews told his readers to keep their eyes on Jesus, so that they could run their race well (Heb 12:1–2).

This is still true for us today: there is no room for competition in the church, for three reasons. First, when we compete with others, we draw attention to ourselves. But we are to draw attention to Jesus, not ourselves. And our own attention should be on him, not on ourselves or other Christians. Second, the church can't accomplish the mission her Lord has given her unless her members work together as a team. We face enough opposition from outside, without having to face opposition from each other. Third, unity among Christians reflects the unity within the Trinity (John 17:21–23). So competition among Christians is contrary to the nature of the God whose nature we're supposed to reflect. For all these reasons, let's focus on running our own race instead of competing with other Christians.

There's no room for competition in the church.

---

* Hudson, *Chariots*.

Today's Reading: Jas 4:1–3

Asking and Getting

FROM CHILDREN SQUABBLING OVER a toy to nations on the battlefield, conflict is everywhere. At the root of most conflicts is frustrated desires. I want something and I don't have it, so I'll take it from you.

In Jas 4:1–3, James offers two answers to the question of why we don't get what we want. The first is deceptively simple: "You do not have because you do not ask" (verse 2 RSV). How much would God give us if we simply asked him for it? Our Father loves us, and he delights in blessing us and meeting our needs. So it pleases him when we ask him for what we need. But asking God for something instead of striving to get it ourselves shows humility, which is difficult for some people. The second reason that James gives for not getting what we want is more challenging: asking with wrong motives (verse 3). It's important that we ask ourselves why we want what we want. God won't give us something that we're just going to use for self-indulgence. But he will provide for us for our legitimate needs. If it's right for us to have it, he'll see that we get it.

The key to avoiding conflict that arises from frustrated desires is to keep God first in our lives. That's why Jesus said, "Do not be anxious, saying, 'What shall we eat?' or 'What shall we drink?' or 'What shall we wear?' For the Gentiles seek all these things; and your heavenly Father knows that you need them all. But seek first his kingdom and his righteousness, and all these things shall be yours as well" (Matt 6:31–33 RSV).

God will meet our needs if we ask him, and ask for the right reasons.

Today's Reading: Rom 12:1–2

Currency of a Life

IN THE FOURTH-SEASON EPISODE of the TV series *Sherlock*, "The Six Thatchers," a woman takes a bullet intended for Sherlock Holmes, sacrificing her life to save his.* In the next episode, "The Lying Detective," he admits to Dr. Watson, "When Mary saved my life she put a value on it. It is a currency I do not know how to spend."** That started me thinking. Jesus sacrificed his life on the cross to save ours. By doing that, he conferred a value on our lives. Paul says that we were bought with a price (1 Cor 6:20, 7:23). 1 Pet 1:19 says that we were redeemed not with perishable things like silver or gold, but with the precious blood of Jesus the Lamb of God. This is the value that God has placed on our lives.

So, how do we spend this currency, this inestimable value God has conferred on our lives? How do we respond to what God has done for us? We must realize that we're not our own. God has bought us with the blood of Jesus. The only right way for us to respond to that is to live under his lordship, living in obedience to him. We also spend the currency of our lives rightly when we pour out our lives in service to God, doing what he has called us to do. We pour our time, effort, and energy into doing whatever God has called us to do, to the best of our ability. This is what Paul means in Rom 12:1–2. Given what God has done for us, our proper response is to offer ourselves in service to him.

Father, you've bought me with the precious blood of Jesus. I am yours, I offer myself to you.

---

* Talalay, dir. *Sherlock*, "Six Thatchers."
** Hurran, dir. *Sherlock*, "Lying Detective".

Today's Reading: Rom 12:4–8

Do What You're Designed For

When I was growing up I had a dog, Shady the black Labrador. Shady loved the water, and she'd go for a swim whenever she got the chance (though I don't remember her ever getting into the bathtub with us). This isn't surprising, because Labradors are bred for the water.

The Labrador retriever originated in the area of Labrador, Canada (now part of the province of Newfoundland and Labrador) in the early 1800s. They were bred to retrieve the birds that hunters had shot, and to help fishermen bring their nets in to shore. So when Shady went swimming, she was doing what she was designed to do.

God has designed each of us for a particular purpose. It might be building or repairing things, it might be music, or sports, or business, or ministry. Whatever it is, God has given you the skills and the characteristics you need to do it (a Labrador's big feet make it easy for them to swim). Another way of saying this is that God has anointed you for what he has called you to do. This doesn't mean, though, that you'll do what God has designed you for without any effort or challenges. You'll still have work to do.

How can we know what God has designed us to do? The easiest way to find that out is to ask ourselves, *What do I have a passion for? What do I enjoy doing? What am I good at?* The answers to these questions will point us to what God has designed us to do. Let's do what God has designed us to do, for other people's good and God's glory.

What has God designed you to do? Your skills, character, and passion will tell you.

Today's Reading: Col 3:12–14

All Dressed Up

GETTING DRESSED IS SOMETHING we all do every day. The New Testament says that we should "put on" certain things. The Greek word which many English Bibles translate "put on," *enduo,* is usually used of putting clothes on. So those translations which say, "clothe yourselves with" have the right idea.

In Col 3:12, Paul says that we are to clothe ourselves with compassion, kindness, humility, gentleness, patience, and forgiveness. On top of these we are to put on love, the belt that holds all the others together. Rom 13:14 and Gal 3:27 say that we are to clothe ourselves with Christ, which might simply be a way of summing up the other things that we are to put on. But what does it mean to clothe ourselves with these godly character qualities? We may note that clothing ourselves is active. Our clothes won't jump onto our bodies by themselves, we have to put them on. So also we have to choose to put on godly character qualities.

Most of us have had the experience of putting something on, and it didn't look right. It was too small, or the color didn't suit us, or the style didn't look good. When that happens, we take that garment off and put something else on. This is also true in the spiritual sense. Bad attitudes like selfishness, greed, anger, bitterness, insincerity, and haughtiness don't suit us as Christians, and they don't look right on us. That's why Paul wrote, "But now put them all away: anger, wrath, malice, slander, and foul talk from your mouth" (Col 3:8 RSV). This is part of putting off the old nature (Eph 4:22; Col 3:9).

Father, I want to be dressed rightly. Help me put on godly character qualities.

Today's Reading: Rom 8:24–25

Hope Without Doubt

POLITICIANS PROMISE THAT THEY can deliver it; people everywhere are looking for it; sometimes it seems to be difficult to find. What is this valued but elusive thing? It is, quite simply, hope.

In the Old Testament, the Hebrew word for "hope" is *batach*. The word implies security and confidence. In the New Testament, the Greek word for "hope" is *elpis*. *Elpis* isn't a weak, wimpy "I hope this will happen;" it's the confident expectation that God will act. Neither word leaves room for doubt.

It's sometimes difficult to keep hope up, because hope involves something absent. As Paul puts it, "Now hope that is seen is no hope at all. Who hopes for what they already have? But if we hope for what we do not yet have, we wait for it patiently" (Rom 8:24–25 NIV). But we can have this kind of hope-without-doubt, not because of who we are, or because of what we're hoping for, but because of whom we're hoping in. Our hope is in a trustworthy God. "God is not human, that he should lie, not a human being, that he should change his mind. Does he speak and then not act? Does he promise and not fulfill?" (Num 23:19 NIV). This is the kind of hope that Abraham held onto, when he believed that God would keep his promise to give Abraham a son (Rom 4:18). And it's the kind of hope we also can have, because God hasn't changed. Whatever we're hoping for, our hope is based in the goodness, faithfulness, and love of God.

May the God of hope fill you with all joy and peace in believing, so that by the power of the Holy Spirit you may abound in hope (Rom 15:13 RSV).

Today's Reading: Rom 7:22-25

The Lion and the Dragon

THE VOYAGE OF THE DAWN TREADER is the fifth book in C.S. Lewis's *The Chronicles of Narnia* series. One of the main characters in this book is annoying schoolboy Eustace Scrubb. Halfway through the story, Eustace (who has been mean to everyone) falls under a spell and is turned into a dragon. Over the next few days, Eustace realizes how bad he has been. He tries to peel off his dragon-skin, with only limited success. He must allow Aslan the great Lion (who symbolizes Christ in Narnia) to peel it off. This process cuts deeper than Eustace wants, and is very painful. But it's only when Aslan peels the dragon-skin off and throws Eustace into a deep pool of water that Eustace is restored.* This illustrates the Biblical principle that we can't change ourselves; we can only change with the help of Christ.

This is Paul's point in Rom 7:14-25. He wants to do what's right, but the sin principle within him prevents him. This is the problem that we all face; on our own, we're powerless against sin. But thank God, everything that needs to be done to free us from sin's power has been done by Jesus Christ (verse 25). It's his work in our lives that transforms us from sinners to saints.

The process of transformation may be painful, because it can cut deeper than we'd like. And it usually takes longer than we want it to. But if we submit to God's working in our lives, the end result will be worth it. God will change us in ways we can't change ourselves, and we'll be far better for it, because we'll look like his Son Jesus (Rom 8:29).

We can't change ourselves; we need Christ's help.

---

* Lewis, *The Chronicles of Narnia*, 473-75

Today's Reading: 2 Cor 2:14–16

What Do You Smell Like?

My cat, Cleopatra, sniffed insistently at my hand. She didn't want me to move my hand to pet her, she wanted to smell it. I don't know what she could smell. But a cat's nose is 9 to 16 times more sensitive than a human nose, and Cleo's nose could detect something that interested her.

In 2 Cor 2:14–16, Paul talks about how Christians should smell. As followers of Jesus, we smell like him, and spread his fragrance wherever we go, like an offering of fragrant incense. This is pleasing to God. To smell like Jesus is to carry his presence around with us, so people can tell that we're his followers. But this smell won't be appealing to everyone. To those who accept God's offer of salvation in Jesus, we're the fragrance of life that calls them to eternal life. But to those who reject God's offer of salvation, we're the stench of death that warns of judgment and eternal death if they persist in their rejection.

People should be able to tell that we're followers of Jesus. It should show in how we talk and act. That's what Peter means when he writes, "But as he who called you is holy, be holy yourselves in all your conduct" (1 Pet 1:15 RSV). And Paul writes, "Follow God's example, therefore, as dearly loved children" (Eph 5:1 NIV). Just as children imitate what they see their parents doing, so we should imitate what we see God, in the form of Jesus, doing. Paul did this, and encouraged his readers to follow his example: "Be imitators of me, as I am of Christ" (1 Cor 11:1 RSV).

Jesus, help me to smell like you. I want to spread your fragrance wherever I go.

Today's Reading: Matt 22:37-40

The Needs of the Many

A GROUP OF ANGRY DEMONSTRATORS blocked an intersection, carrying signs that read INDIVIDUAL RIGHTS and NO MORE RESTRICTIONS. But an equally angry group of people opposed them. A man shouted, "I have both diabetes and asthma. If I get COVID it will kill me. What about my right to life?" A woman called out, "My mother's old and frail, I look after her. What if I give her the virus?" It's a debate that has wound its ugly way around the world in the past year or so. As I've watched it, I've remembered a *Star Trek* phrase: "The needs of the many outweigh the needs of the needs of the few, or the one."*

Actually, this idea is much older than *Star Trek*. In Matt 22:39 Jesus said that the second-greatest commandment is to love one's neighbor as oneself. He was quoting Lev 19:18. This is a foundational principle of Judaism as well as Christianity. Even the Pharisees wouldn't have disagreed with Jesus on this point! Paul is thinking of the same principle in Phil 2:3-4, "Do nothing from selfishness or conceit, but in humility count others better than yourselves. Let each of you look not only to his own interests, but also to the interests of others" (RSV). This, he says, is the example that Jesus gave us (verses 5-12). Rather than hold on to his rights as God the Son, He laid them aside temporarily for our sake. As his disciples, we should imitate him (1 Cor 11:1). Let's follow his example of being willing to put other people's needs ahead of our own.

Sometimes loving our neighbor as ourselves means being willing to set aside our individual rights for the good of others.

---

* This phrase, used several times in film and TV versions of the series, was first used in Meyer, *Khan*.

Today's Reading: Matt 7:24–27

Building on Two Foundations

THE LEANING TOWER OF PISA is actually the bell tower of the cathedral of the city of Pisa, Italy. Completed in 1372, it's one of Italy's most famous tourist attractions. But do you know why the Tower leans? It leans because the builders laid the tower's foundation half on rock and half on soft soil. They reasoned that if half the building's foundation were on rock, the foundation would still be strong enough to support the entire building. They were wrong; by the time the second story was completed, one side of the building was already sinking into the soft soil. In fact, if modern experts hadn't taken action, the tower would probably have collapsed by now, with possibly disastrous consequences.

This reminds me of the person who builds only part of the foundation of their life on Jesus. The person who, as we sometimes say, has one foot in the world and one foot in the kingdom. This is not a position that we can stay in for very long, because, as Jesus warns in Matt 6:24, "No one can serve two masters" (RSV). Anyone who tries to do that will inevitably come to love one master and hate the other. If we try to build on two foundations, it leaves a door open for the enemy to get at us and destroy us. The Spirit of God and the world will always pull us in opposite directions, and we'll inevitably fall apart. God wants our entire allegiance, not a half-hearted commitment. Let's not allow anything else to take the place in our hearts and lives that belongs to God alone.

If we try to stand with one foot in the world and one foot in the kingdom, we will fall apart.

Today's Reading: Heb 10:24–25

Safety in Numbers

WHEN LIONESSES, OR TIGERS, or wolves attack a herd of gazelles, or deer, or whatever, they try to cut an individual out of the herd. An animal on its own is easier to take down. An isolated animal is easy prey for the enemy.

The same is true of Christians. Our enemy the devil prowls around like a lion on the hunt, looking for someone he can devour (1 Pet 5:8). An important defence against him is to stay closely connected to the Body of Christ, the church. It's important that we meet regularly with other Christians. This was the habit of the early church, whether they gathered in each other's homes or in the Jerusalem temple (Acts 2:42,46). And it's as necessary for us now as it was for them at that time.

The church is where we can "stir up one another to love and good works" (verse 24 RSV) that is, encourage one another to stay on track with God and live the way Christians should live. It's also where we learn about God from those who are more experienced in the things of God than we are. This is important if we are to avoid falling into false teaching. It's easier for us to stay on track with God if we're around people who are also on track with God. It isn't always easy to be godly in an ungodly world. And the closer we get to the day of Jesus' return, the more difficult it will get. So it's all the more important that we stick together to encourage and protect each other. This is the meaning of Heb 10:25. There's safety in numbers.

Being closely connected to the church is the believer's defence against the enemy.

Today's Reading: 1 Cor 1:26–29

The Weak Things

AT THE END OF *THE TWO TOWERS*, the second part of J.R.R. Tolkien's *The Lord of the Rings*, Frodo is stung by the giant spider Shelob. Sam, finding himself alone, must decide what to do. Should he take the Ring and try to complete the Quest, or stay by Frodo and probably die with him? Sam doesn't consider himself the right person for heroic deeds. But he says to himself, "You haven't put yourself forward, you've been put forward. And as for not being the right and proper person, why, Mr. Frodo wasn't, as you might say, nor Mr. Bilbo. They didn't choose themselves."* This illustrates the principle that Paul sets out in 1 Cor 1:26–29. God uses what seems weak and unimportant in the eyes of the world to accomplish his purposes.

Paul reminds the Corinthians that while some of them are well-educated, influential or of noble birth, most of them aren't. God doesn't choose people because of their wisdom, wealth or rank in this world. Rather he chooses those whom the world overlooks or disregards. He does this so that he gets the glory, and no human. The best-known example of this from Scripture is David. No one, including David's own family, thought much of him while he was a teenager tending his father's sheep (1 Sam 16:1–13). But David became one of Israel's greatest kings. God used David to defeat Israel's enemies and enlarge her territory. This principle still applies today. God can use us even if we don't have status, power, or money. He uses people who are aware of their weaknesses and rely on him for strength. Those are the people through whom God does great things.

God uses people whom the world disregards to carry out his purposes.

---

* Tolkien, *Rings*, 732.

Today's Reading: Job 42:1–6

Why?

CALLERS TO THE PRAYER LINE often ask me questions beginning with "Why." Why did God take my spouse away from me? Why is God allowing this person to treat me like this? Why did God allow me to lose my job? These questions have a common theme: the people asking them want God to give them an explanation.

One can hardly think of this subject without thinking of the book of Job. Job repeatedly asks God to explain why he, Job, is suffering as he is (Job 13:3; 30:20; 31:35). But for most of the book God is silent. When he does speak, God shows Job that he's better able to run the universe than Job is. Instead of an explanation, God gives Job a revelation of himself. That turns out to be all Job needs, and he repents of his defiant self-righteousness. That's what he means when he says, "My ears had heard of you, but now my eyes have seen you. Therefore I despise myself and repent in dust and ashes" (Job 42:5–6 NIV).

This is what God wants for us. We want an explanation; God wants to give us a revelation of himself. And we can know for certain what Job could see only a hint of. Because God's ultimate revelation of himself is in Jesus (John 1:18). I'm reminded of the apostle Thomas, whose doubt and fear were resolved when he saw the risen Jesus (John 20:22–24). That was enough for Thomas, just as seeing God in the whirlwind was enough for Job. God is better at running the universe than we could ever hope to be, so let's trust him and let him do his job.

We want God to give us an explanation; God wants to give us a revelation of himself.

Today's Reading: Eph 5:15–17

What We Do in Life

NEAR THE BEGINNING OF the movie *Gladiator*, General Maximus, encouraging his men before they go into a major battle, says, "Brothers, what we do in life echoes in eternity."[*] In other words, if they fight well, they will earn glory for themselves; if they die in the battle, they will go to Elysium, the place of the heroic dead.

The Bible indicates that what we do here has lasting consequences, both for this life and for eternity. So it's important to watch how we live and make the most of our time. This is Paul's point in Eph 5:15–17. In 1 Cor 3:12–15 Paul reminds us to make sure that what we do here will stand in eternity. We all have the same twenty-four hours in each day. The people who make a difference for God in the world do so because they make wise use of their time. How do we spend our time: playing on the internet, watching too much TV, or engaging in gossip with friends? Or in taking time with God, serving him by serving others, and doing our job diligently? There's a time for rest, and a time for play; we need these things too. But let's keep it in balance. Let's not waste our time on earth doing things that won't count for eternity. I know how easy it is to get distracted by things that pull our attention away from where it should be. But let's keep our primary focus on doing what God has called us to do, whatever that may be. We honor the God who made time by spending our time wisely, doing things that count for eternity.

Let's spend our time here doing what counts for eternity.

---

[*] Scott, *Gladiator*.

Today's Reading: Jer 29:11

Facing the Future

SOMETIMES I TALK WITH CHRISTIANS who have consulted fortune tellers or had tarot card readings, and they want to repent of doing so. Their reason for dabbling in the occult like this is always the same: they want to know what their future holds. God has told us not to be involved in the occult (see, e.g. Lev 19:26; Deut 18:10–12; 1 Sam 15:23), because occult practices mess with dangerous spiritual forces.

It's understandable that people would want to know what their future holds. The future is unknown to us, and we humans don't like the unknown. It frightens us, because we can't control it. Knowledge is power. We feel that if we knew what the future will bring, we could control it. But that isn't what God wants for us. He wants us to trust him with the future.

A famous verse on this subject is Jer 29:11: "For I know the plans I have for you, says the LORD, plans for welfare and not for evil, to give you a future and a hope" (RSV). We may notice that God says, "I know," he doesn't say, "I'll tell you." God doesn't promise to tell us our future. Rather he assures us that he knows what he's doing, even when we don't know what he's doing. God wants us to trust him with the future, which we can't see but he can. Faith is about things *not* seen (Heb 11:1, emphasis added). This isn't easy. But God is trustworthy. He loves us, and wants good things for us. All things are under his control. We can trust him with the future.

We don't know what the future holds, but we do know the God who holds the future, and we can trust him.

Today's Reading: 1 Cor 12:12–20

Different, And Needed

EVERYONE KNOWS THAT THE HUMAN body is made up of different parts. Everyone knew it in the apostle Paul's time, too. Maybe that's why God gave Paul the image of the church as the body of Christ: it's an image anyone can understand. "The body of Christ" is distinctively Paul's phrase—outside Paul's letters, it appears only in Hebrews (twice) and 1 Peter (once). In 1 Cor 12:12-25, Paul says that each part of the human body is different, but they all form one whole. Each part needs to be functioning properly for the body to be healthy. So each part is valuable and needed.

It's the same way, Paul says, in the body of Christ. Members of the body aren't all alike. But we're all needed. It's easy to fall into the trap of wishing that our fellow church members were more like us, because then they would be easier to get along with. But in fact it's our differences that make the body of Christ work. It's when the members of the body of Christ use their various gifts and skills that all the body's needs are met. Welcoming those who are different from us, but have "a faith of equal standing with ours" (2 Pet 1:1 RSV) will help keep the church healthy. This isn't always easy; we need the help of the Holy Spirit to get along and work together. With his help we can rejoice in our differences instead of resenting them. If we do, our individual lives will be richer and the body of Christ will be healthier.

Jesus, Head of the body of Christ, help the members of your body to bring our differences and work together, so all the body's needs are met.

Today's Reading: John 16:23–27

In Jesus' Name

FOR CENTURIES, CHRISTIANS HAVE ENDED their prayers with the phrase, "In Jesus' name." It's become so customary that we can miss its significance. What does it mean to pray in Jesus' name?

In Scripture a person's name sums up their character and actions, and represents them. So when we ask the Father for something in Jesus' name, it's as if Jesus was asking, not us. TLB captures this idea with its version of verse 26: "You will present your petitions over my signature." Jesus has given us permission to use his name when we make requests in prayer; this is a great privilege.

We can draw two conclusions from our permission to ask for things in Jesus' name. First, we can be certain that what we ask in Jesus' name the Father will do, if it's in line with his will. In a letter John wrote, "This is the confidence we have in approaching God: that if we ask anything according to his will, he hears us. And if we know that he hears us—whatever we ask—we know that we have what we asked of him" (1 John 5:14–15 NIV).

Second, we must not misuse this gracious permission and make foolish or self-indulgent requests. This is one reason for unanswered prayer. "When you ask, you do not receive, because you ask with wrong motives, that you may spend what you get on your pleasures" (Jas 4:3 NIV). If Jesus wouldn't ask for it, neither should we. If we use the name of Jesus rightly in prayer, we can use it with confidence and trust.

Thank you Jesus for graciously giving us permission to go to the Father in your name. This is a great privilege that you have given us.

Today's Reading: Josh 1:5–9

"As I Was With Moses…"

THE BEGINNING OF THE BOOK of Joshua marks a turning point in Israel's history. The generation that had left Egypt had all died, and it was time for their children to enter the Promised Land. And there was another change too: among those who had died was Moses, who had led them that far. The responsibility for actually leading Israel across the Jordan River and into the Promised Land fell to Joshua, who had been Moses' assistant.

Joshua chapter 1 doesn't say explicitly how Joshua was feeling at that moment. But from the number of times that God told Joshua to be strong and courageous (Josh 1:6,7,9) we may fairly conclude that Joshua was feeling anything but strong and courageous! But God assured him, "As I was with Moses, so I will be with you; I will never leave you nor forsake you" (Josh 1:5 NIV). That's why Joshua could be strong and courageous. He wasn't doing it alone, God was with him. God made the same commitment to Joshua as he had made to Moses (see Exod 3:12). God wasn't telling Joshua to change. He was telling Joshua that he, God, hadn't changed.

This is still true; God still hasn't changed. He has made the same promise to his people now that he made then. The God who was with Moses, Joshua, and the apostles is also with us. He has promised that he is with us always (Matt 28:20) and that he will never leave us or forsake us (Deut 31:6; Heb 13:5). So we also can be strong and courageous, because the Lord our God is with us wherever we go (verse 9).

The God who was with Moses, Joshua, and the apostles is also with us.

Today's Reading: Rom 5:15–19

The Last Adam

A TURNING POINT IN J.R.R TOLKIEN'S *The Lord of the Rings* comes when the wizard Gandalf the Grey, resurrected as Gandalf the White, is reunited with his friends Aragorn, Legolas, and Gimli. At first they think that he is the evil wizard Saruman. Once he has convinced them of who he is, he says, "I *am* Saruman, one might almost say, Saruman as he should have been."* There are several ways in which Gandalf resembles Christ, and this is one of them. For one might say that Christ is Adam, Adam as he should have been.

This is the comparison that Paul makes in Rom 5:15–19 and 1 Cor 15:21–22. It's interesting that Jesus has his final struggle with temptation in a garden, the Garden of Gethsemane. Adam was also tempted in a garden, the Garden of Eden. But while Adam failed and gave in to temptation, Jesus didn't. Adam disobeyed God and did the only thing that God had told him not to do (Gen 3:1–6). Jesus walked in submissive obedience to his Father, not only in Gethsemane but throughout his time on earth (John 5:19; 8:28–29; 14:31). This humility is the opposite of the pride that Adam showed in thinking that he knew better than God, which led to his sin of disobedience. Adam's act of disobedience has affected every one of his descendants to this day; but Jesus by his act of obedience undid the consequences of what Adam had done. Jesus lived the way Adam should have lived, in closeness and obedience to God. Thus he not only modelled for us how we should live, but empowers us to live that way too.

Jesus is Adam as he should have been.

---

* Tolkien, *Rings*, 495.

Today's Reading: Lam 3:21–24

God's Endless Mercies

A WOMAN PHONED ME IN the middle of the night, distraught. "I've just sinned," she sobbed, "and God can't forgive me because he's run out of mercy for today, and he won't make a new batch of mercy until the morning." I knew that she was referring to Lam 3:23. But she misunderstood that verse.

That God's mercies are new every morning doesn't mean that God runs out of mercy during the night. That would make verse 24 disagree with verse 23, which says that God's mercies never come to an end. Rather the two verses say the same thing in two different ways, as is often done in Hebrew poetry (for other examples of this see, e.g., Pss 5:1–2; 25:4–5; 73:4–5; 135:6–7). In other words, that the Lord's mercies are new every morning means that they never come to an end.

Jeremiah and his people were going through a difficult time, but Jeremiah found hope in remembering that God's mercies never end. We may notice the phrase in verse 21, "this I call to mind."(RSV) There's something deliberate about this. In the midst of overwhelming anguish, Jeremiah found hope by choosing to recall God's unending mercies. This is how he fought back against despair. We can do the same thing today, because God hasn't changed. He's still loving and merciful. He's still faithful to his people. So like Jeremiah we can have hope in tough times by remembering God's faithfulness. It's not always easy to do that. But if we do, we'll find that God is still loving and merciful.

Thank you Lord that you never run out of mercy. I never run out of need for your mercy. Thank you that your mercies never end. Great is your faithfulness!

Today's Reading: Col 3:22–25

Bring Your A-Game

GOD WANTS US TO do our best, whatever we're doing. This is one of the things that Paul means in Col 3:17, "And whatever you do, in word or deed, do everything in the name of the Lord Jesus, giving thanks to God the Father through him" (RSV). Everything we do, we are to do as God's representatives and for his glory. Similarly in verse 23, Paul says, "Whatever you do, work at it with all your heart, as working for the Lord, not for human masters" (NIV). In the context, Paul is talking to slaves. But his advice applies to employees today, too. We are to do the best job we can at work. And not just when the boss is looking (this is the meaning of verse 22b RSV, "not with eyeservice, as men-pleasers"). This isn't easy when we have a bad boss (I know, I've been there). But it's easier if we see ourselves as working for our ultimate boss, the Lord, not just for our earthly supervisor. It doesn't matter whether the job is cleaning, teaching, serving food or rocket science. Every job is valuable and worth doing well.

Doing a mediocre job at something when we're capable of doing it well is not honoring to God. He wants our best. As my father used to say, "If it's worth doing, it's worth doing right." Not that God expects us to be perfect. He knows that we won't be perfect until we get to heaven. But we honor him by doing the best we can. He's pleased with that.

Lord, help me to honor you by doing the best I can, at everything I do. You don't expect me to be perfect, but you're pleased when I do my best.

Today's Reading: Rom 7:14–25

Superhero

I ENJOY A GOOD SUPERHERO MOVIE. And from the box-office success of movies from Marvel Studios and DC Entertainment, it appears I'm not the only one. People have always enjoyed superhero stories, from Samson and Herakles (also called Hercules) in the ancient world, to Superman, Batman, Wonder Woman, and other comic-book creations. Why are superhero stories so popular? I think it's because we all feel a need for someone stronger than we are to come alongside us and help us. We all feel that there are things that we just aren't strong enough to deal with, enemies we aren't strong enough to defeat.

The ultimate superhero, of course, is Jesus. He came to earth and rescued us from a danger far greater than any peril that ever threatened Lois Lane: our bondage to sin. Paul wrote, "While we were still weak, at the right time Christ died for the ungodly" (Rom 5:6 RSV). In Rom 7:14–25 Paul writes about his inward struggle with sin. He wants to do what is right, but the sin principle within him prevents him from doing it. This is a dilemma that we inherited from our first parents, Adam and Eve (Rom 5:12–15). Finally Paul says in frustration, "What a wretched man I am! Who will rescue me from this body that is subject to death?" (Rom 7:24 NIV). But he already knows the answer: through Jesus, God has already provided the means for our rescue. By his death and resurrection Jesus has rescued us from sin and set us free from it. So we don't need to, and shouldn't, live under the power of sin any longer (Rom 6:1–14).

Jesus our Hero has rescued us from the power of sin, so we can live free from its power.

Today's Reading: John 17:20-23

"That All May Be One"

A FLOCK OF BIRDS FLEW across the sky in a black cloud, swooping and swirling, forming liquid shapes but always staying together. As I watched, I wondered how they stayed in that kind of unity.

God wants unity among his people too. In John 17:20-23, Jesus prayed that his disciples would be one, just as he and the Father are one. That is, we are to have the same kind of unity as the Father and the Son have. This unity will show the world that God sent Jesus. In other words, our unity is to be a witness about God to an unbelieving world. This is what Jesus meant when he said, "By this everyone will know that you are my disciples, if you love one another" (John 13:35 NIV). We can show the world what God's love can do to unite people of differing racial, national, and socioeconomic groups. And there has never been a time when the world needed to see that more. Around the world, nations are tearing themselves, and each other, apart. If we demonstrate to the world what real unity looks like, we can bring healing where now there is only division and hurt.

Paul scolded the Corinthians for their disunity (1 Cor 1:10-13), and, sadly, things haven't changed. There are, and have always been, differences among Christians. But we have more things in common than we have differences. It's time for us to focus more on what we agree on than on what we don't agree on. We're called to "one hope . . . one Lord, one faith, one baptism; one God and Father of all." (Eph 4:4-6 RSV).

Christian unity shows the world what God can do to unite people from differing backgrounds.

Today's Reading: Phil 1:6

A Work in Progress

SEVERAL YEARS AGO, the house behind mine was torn down and a new one built. It was interesting to watch the process. Over a period of months, what looked like a demolition site was transformed into a comfortable home.

One of my favorite Bible verses is Phil 1:6, "He who began a good work in you will bring it to completion at the day of Jesus Christ" (RSV). Perhaps it's a favorite because I'm often disappointed in myself. It's encouraging to remember that God is still working on me. That as long as I'm growing spiritually, he's pleased with me. He doesn't want me to stay as I am, but he loves me as I am, and that never changes.

God is at work in the life of every believer. He's at work even in those seasons when we don't seem to be changing very much. Little by little, God is changing us into the people he wants us to be, raising us from one level of glory to another (2 Cor 3:18) and making us like his Son Jesus. This is his will for us (Rom 8:29). But it isn't always easy or comfortable, and it isn't a quick fix. It takes time; but God is never in a hurry. This means that we need to be patient with ourselves and with others, because all of us are works in progress. None of us is perfect, and we won't be perfect until we get to heaven. God won't stop working in us until then. I'm reminded of a saying that went around the church in the 1970's: "Please Be Patient, God Has Not Finished With Me Yet."

Father, help me to be patient with myself and others, because we're all works in progress.

Today's Reading: 1 Pet 2:4–8

The Church Endures

IN THE CLASSIC STAR *Trek* season 2 episode "Bread and Circuses" the *Enterprise* crew search for a missing freighter. They find the surviving members of its crew on a planet whose culture is similar to that of twentieth-century Earth–but on this planet, the Roman Empire never fell. Kirk, Spock, and McCoy are befriended by a group of runaway slaves known as the "children of the sun." Near the end of the story, Lt. Uhura says that she has been listening to the Empire's radio broadcasts. The Empire has been trying to ridicule the belief of the "children of the sun"–but they can't. Uhura has realized that the "children of the sun" worship not a star, but the Son of God. The "children of the sun" are Christians, children of the Son.[*] The message that I get from this is that the church endures, in spite of her opponents.

Jesus said that hell itself would not overpower the church, because he would build it (Matt 16:18). He himself is the church's cornerstone, and the apostles are her foundation (Eph 2:20). There's no beginning more stable than this. And we are living stones, being built on this foundation into a spiritual house by God himself (1 Pet 2:5). The Holy Spirit is the mortar that holds us together. This is a building that's built to last! The church has suffered religious and political opposition since her beginning. But history has shown time and time again that opposition only makes the church grow. Nothing can knock her down, because she is built and held together by the power of God himself.

The church endures in spite of her opponents, because she is built by God and Jesus is her cornerstone.

---

[*] Senensky, *Trek*, "Circuses."

Today's Reading: Jas 3:2–8

Can't Undo

A WOMAN PHONED GOOGLE TECH support in tears. She'd sent an angry email to her boss a few minutes previously, and had realized that it was a mistake. But once an email is sent in Gmail, it can't be undone. On a lower-tech level, once we say something to someone, whether face-to-face or over the phone, we can't unsay it. So it's important to think before we speak.

This is what is meant by Prov 13:3 NIV, "Those who guard their lips preserve their lives, but those who speak rashly will come to ruin." And Jas 1:19–20 NIV says, "My dear brothers and sisters, take note of this: Everyone should be quick to listen, slow to speak and slow to become angry, because human anger does not produce the righteousness that God desires." Words have power, and we can use our words for good or for evil, to help or to hurt. So it's important that we think before we speak. In fact, thinking before we speak is a mark of spiritual maturity. James says that anyone who has control over their tongue is spiritually mature, and has control over every other area of their life as well (Jas 3:2). We can't do this on our own. As James points out, no human can tame the tongue (Jas 3:8). But we have the Holy Spirit in us to help us, and one of the fruit of the Spirit is self-control (Gal. 5:23). So with the Holy Spirit's help, we can refrain from saying something that will be unhelpful to someone else.

Lord, I know that once I say something I can't unsay it, so I need to control my tongue. But I can't do that without your help. Help me think before I speak.

Today's Reading: Jonah 1:1–3; 3:1–3

God of the Second Chance

A MAN CALLED ME ON the Prayer Line, saying that several years ago God had told him to do something and he hadn't done it. Now he felt that God had given up on him because of his disobedience. Had rejected him. He felt ashamed and condemned. In fact I get calls on this subject quite often. But the feeling behind them is based on a lie from Satan, the lie that we have only one chance with God. But God doesn't give up on us like that.

God didn't give up on Jonah. God called Jonah to go to Nineveh and call the city to repentance. But Jonah didn't want to go, so he ran in the opposite direction (Jonah 1:1–3). God called him a second time, and this time he went (Jonah 3:1–3). His obedience shows that he repented. So God used Jonah in the way that he intended to all along.

Jesus didn't give up on his disciple Peter either. The night that Jesus was arrested, Peter denied that he knew Jesus. But after his resurrection, Jesus restored Peter to a place of leadership (John 21:15–19).

There's nothing that God won't forgive those who genuinely repent. If you've stumbled and sinned, you can always turn back to God. 1 John 1:9 RSV says, "If we confess our sins, [God] is faithful and just, and will forgive our sins and cleanse us from all unrighteousness." The fact that my caller phoned me told me that God was still calling him, just as he called Jonah a second time. God hasn't given up on you. He'll give you a second chance if you ask him to.

God gives those who repent a second chance.

Today's Reading: Ps 36:5–9

Leap of Faith

NEAR THE END OF THE MOVIE *Indiana Jones and the Last Crusade*, Indy must overcome three obstacles to find the Holy Grail, the cup of the Last Supper, because drinking from it will heal his seriously injured father. The last obstacle is "a leap from the lion's mouth." Indy realizes that what is meant isn't the chasm that he's standing at, but a leap of faith. Meanwhile his father whispers to himself, "You must believe, boy; you must believe."* I couldn't help wondering, Faith in what, or whom? Believe in what, or whom? It looks as if Indy succeeds by putting his faith in himself; but is this a viable answer in real life?

Most of us have failed at something we've tried. Or we've promised ourselves we'd do something, and haven't done it. We feel we've let ourselves down. Or other people have let us down. We've learned the hard way not to put too much faith in others, or even ourselves. God is the only one who won't let us down. He's not a human being, that he would lie or change his mind (Num 23:19). What he says, he will do. That doesn't mean that he'll do everything we want him to. But he always keeps his promises. God is committed to his people, and he cares for them. That's why the palmist could write, "I will say of the Lord, 'He is my refuge and my fortress, my God, in whom I trust' . . . He will cover you with his feathers, and under his wings you will find refuge; his faithfulness is a shield and rampart" (Ps 91:2, 4 NIV).

Father, you're the only one who will never let me down. I put my faith in you.

---

* Spielberg, *Last Crusade*.

Today's Reading: Ps 136:1–3, 23–26

God's Covenant Care

It happened many years ago, but it was a lesson I'll never forget. I was a graduate student, and like many grad students, I was struggling financially. One day I was complaining to the Lord about the state of my bank account. Minutes after I finished, a neighbor knocked on my door. Christmas was coming, and in her baking she had ended up with an extra fruitcake. I lived on that fruitcake for the next week, because it was about all that I had in my fridge. The timing didn't escape my notice, either. God had provided for me even as I was complaining about my lack.

God is merciful, even when we don't deserve it (if we deserved it, it wouldn't be mercy). He also provided for the Israelites in spite of their constant complaining (see, e.g., Exod 16:11–16). This is still true, because God hasn't changed. He has made a covenant with his people, and he won't break it, because such faithlessness is not in his nature. This is what Paul meant when he wrote, "If we are faithless, he remains faithful—for he cannot deny himself." (2 Tim 2:13 RSV). God is committed to us, and that commitment is dependent on God's character, not our behavior.

Not that we should presume on God's covenant faithfulness. Jeremiah warned Israel not to assume that they could sin just because the temple was in Jerusalem (Jer 7:1–10). In the New Testament, Paul says that we're dead to sin and shouldn't live in it any longer (Rom 6:1–4). But we can be glad that God is faithful, even when we aren't.

Thank you Lord that you care for your people even when we don't deserve it. Thank you for your covenant-keeping love and faithfulness.

Today's Reading: Deut 29:29

Secret Things, Revealed Things

IN THE THIRD-SEASON CLASSIC *Star Trek* episode "For the World is Hollow and I Have Touched the Sky," the *Enterprise* crew encounters an asteroid which is actually a spaceship, a hollow sphere. The people of Yonada don't realize that they're on a spaceship which their ancestors boarded ten thousand years previously, headed for a new world. Their ancestors have hidden on the ship the information that they will need when they reach their destination. Their leader, the High Priestess Natira, isn't overly eager to learn their ancestors' secrets; it's enough for her to know that they will understand everything when they get to their new home. Later, she says that she now understands their ancestors' great purpose; in other words, she understands enough to know what she must do now. *

We humans tend to want all the answers, now. We want to know why certain things happen and what the future holds. But faith involves trust. It involves unanswered questions. There are some things that we don't need to know. We certainly should get into God's written word, the Bible, and long to know its secrets. And I for one find that mining its rich treasures takes time and effort enough! Unlike the Book of the People of Yonada, the Bible contains the "revealed things;" it belongs "to us and to our children forever." The Bible holds all the truth that God wants us to know for here and now. Let it be enough for us that when we get to heaven we'll understand all the things that we don't understand now. Meanwhile, we can understand God's purpose for us here.

The Bible gives us all we need to know for life here; the rest we'll understand when we get to heaven.

---

* Leader, *Trek*, "Hollow."

Today's Reading: Col 3:12–15

When Mordor Laughs

"COME, COME . . . WE ARE ALL friends here, or should be. For the laughter of Mordor will be our only reward, if we quarrel." This line from J.R.R. Tolkein's *The Lord of the Rings* is what Gandalf says to Háma the door guard, when Háma, thinking that Gandalf and his party might be enemies, tries to refuse them entry into the hall of King Théoden.* This line touches on an important theme in *The Lord of the Rings*: the Free Peoples must set aside their differences and work together if they are going to defeat the enemy.

Recently some of my colleagues and I had a conversation about the debates that have divided the church recently. I said, "The enemy must be laughing when he sees this." What's true for the Free Peoples of Middle-Earth is also true for the church.

Disunity has been a problem in the church since her early days (1 Cor 1:10–13). In Jesus' prayer in John 17, our unity reflects the unity of the Father and the Son, and is a witness to the world (John 17:21–23). But the preceding verses hint that our unity is also a defence against opposition from the world (verses 11–19). The enemy is the only one who benefits when we argue among ourselves. It distracts us from standing against him, and from serving God and advancing God's kingdom. This is especially true when we allow ourselves to be divided about things that aren't that important. When interacting with our brothers and sisters in Christ, unity in the body of Christ is to be our referee, because God has called us to peace (Col 3:15).

When we argue among ourselves, especially about minor things, the enemy is the only one who benefits.

---

* Tolkien, *Rings*, 511.

Today's Reading: Matt 18:21–22

Seventy Times Seven

AN ISSUE WHICH COMES up frequently in ministry is that of forgiveness. People want to know how to respond when they've been hurt. What does God want them to do then?

Jesus dealt with this in the last section of Matt 18. Peter came to Jesus and asked how many times he should forgive someone who had sinned against him. As many as seven times? Peter probably thought he was being generous, to be willing to forgive seven times. And he probably wasn't prepared for Jesus' challenging answer: not just seventy times, but seventy times seven. Jesus then expanded on this answer with the parable of the Unforgiving Servant (Matt 18:23–35).

Forgiving is one of the most challenging parts of the Christian life. It goes against our human inclination to hold onto hurt and to want revenge. But Jesus calls on us to let him act on our behalf. It may be helpful to know that forgiving someone for what they did doesn't mean that what they did was okay. When we forgive, we put the situation into God's hands, which allows God to deal with the situation. It also releases us from the power of that hurt. Once we forgive, the offender no longer has any power over us.

It may also help to remember that however much we forgive, God has forgiven us more. This is the meaning of the parable of the Unforgiving Servant. It's also what Paul meant when he wrote, "Bear with each other and forgive one another if any of you has a grievance against someone. Forgive as the Lord forgave you" (Col 3:13 NIV). In forgiving, we not only obey God but follow his example.

Father, I forgive anyone who has hurt me, just as you've forgiven me.

Today's Reading: Ps 139:13–18

Custom-Built, by Hand

THE CLASSIC BRITISH TV SERIES *The Prisoner* (1967–1968) is about a senior MI6 agent who resigns after an argument with a superior. He returns to his London home, but is kidnapped and finds himself in a place known only as the Village, a place which looks like a British holiday resort. In the episode "Many Happy Returns," the ex-agent (known only as "No. 6") escapes and returns to London, to find someone else living in his house and using his car, a Lotus 7. He's certain that the car is his, because he knows the license plate number and the number on the engine. "I know every nut and bolt and cog," he insists. "I built it with my own hands!"*

God knows every muscle and bone and organ in our bodies. He knows our every thought and feeling and intention, because he built each of us with his own hands, physically and emotionally, to his own design. He knows you through and through, inside and out, even better than you know yourself. And here's the amazing thing: God loves you, weaknesses and all. In fact, if we give our weaknesses to God, he'll turn them into our greatest blessings. Into the very things that he can use most for his glory. His grace is sufficient for us, because his strength is made perfect in our weakness. So when we're weak, that's when we're strong (2 Cor 12:9-10). You're no surprise to God, and you aren't a mistake. He knew what he was getting when he called you. He has a plan and a purpose and a call on your life, and he has custom-designed you to carry it out.

God knows us inside and out, because he built us with his own hands.

---

* Serf, *Prisoner*, "Returns."

Today's Reading: 1 John 5:14–15

On Prayer

PEOPLE SOMETIMES ASK ME about prayer. Prayer is a key part of the Christian life. We can't fully discuss this important subject here, but I'd like to share a few thoughts.

Prayer doesn't have to be difficult or complicated. Prayer is simply a conversation between a believer and God. We can talk with God the way we talk with our best friend, who knows us and cares about us. There's no need for fancy language, as if we could impress him that way. We can be honest with him, too, because he already knows our hearts and minds. Let's also remember that a real conversation involves listening as well as talking. When we talk with God, let's be careful to listen for what he has to say to us. I confess, listening to God is an area in which I need to grow!

We can also be sure that God always hears our prayers. When God doesn't answer prayer right away, that doesn't mean that he isn't listening. Nowhere is Scripture does God promise that he'll always do what we want him to do, when we want him to do it. But he always hears us. And if what we're asking is in line with his will, we can be sure that he'll hear and answer (1 John 5:14-15).

We may also say that prayer isn't a right or a duty, but a privilege. The Ruler of the universe allows us to bring our needs and concerns to him! But it's only through Jesus that we have access to God in prayer. That's why we pray in Jesus' name. Let's not ignore the privilege and power of prayer.

Thank you Father for the privilege of prayer. Thank you for hearing me when I call.

Today's Reading: Ps 133

We Are Family

THE TV SERIES NUMB3RS is about a young math genius who uses his mathematical ability to help his brother, an FBI agent, solve crimes. One of the themes that runs through the entire series is the relationship between the two brothers, Charlie and Don. The Eppes brothers don't always agree, they aren't alike. They sometimes compete with each other. But their relationship remains sound. Blood, as they say, is thicker than water.

The church is also a family. In some sections of the church, Christians call each other "brother" and "sister," and this is no accident. It was also the custom of the early church (see, e.g., 1Cor 14:6,26; Heb 3:1,12; Jas 1:2,9). And the New Testament refers to the church as a household (Gal 6:10; Eph 2:19; 1 Tim 5:15). We're brothers and sisters to every member of the church, made so by our common relationship with God through Jesus. So let's treat each other like brothers and sisters should. Not squabbling among ourselves or competing with each other, but supporting, encouraging, and helping each other. Which doesn't mean we must agree on everything.

We may also say that young siblings often squabble among themselves. A certain amount of such sibling rivalry is normal—for children. Grown-up siblings should be able to do better (though I know it isn't that way in some families). This is as true in the church as it is in the family. This is what Paul meant when he scolded the Corinthians for their many factions; this, he says, is a sign of spiritual immaturity (1 Cor 3:1–3). Let's build each other up and live in harmony, like brothers and sisters in Christ should.

Father, we're brothers and sisters in Christ, so help us act like it.

Today's Reading: Rom 6:6–11

Free!

My all-time favourite hymn is Charles Wesley's "And can it be that I should gain," written in 1738. The fourth verse says,

> Long my imprisoned spirit lay
> Fast bound in sin and nature's night;
> Thine eye diffused a quickening ray,
> I woke, the dungeon flamed with light;
> My chains fell off, my heart was free;
> I rose, went forth, and followed Thee.

We who are in Christ are free from sin's power. We are dead to sin, so it has no power over us. This is what Paul means in Rom 6:6-11. In Christ we are free from sin, we don't have to allow it to have power over us any longer. In Christ we are free to live the way God wants us to, because he gives us the power to live his way. This is good news for those who struggle with temptation; you don't have to give in to it. God provides a way out (1 Cor 10:13) and gives us the power to take it. Sometimes the way out is a literal one—I don't know how many times I've had to leave a kitchen to avoid eating something I shouldn't! And I've often prayed with someone who has reached out for prayer in a moment of temptation. It's also good news for those who struggle with sin of any kind, whether it be an addiction, a wrong attitude that we know we need to let go of, or behavior that we know needs to change. God will give us the power to give up what is wrong and choose what is right. We aren't trapped in sin anymore; we are free.

In Christ we don't have to let sin have power over us. We are free to live God's way.

Today's Reading: Luke 17:5-6

A Little is Enough

CALLERS OFTEN PHONE THE PRAYER LINE saying, "Pray that I'll have more faith," or, "Ask God to give me greater faith." Whatever they're dealing with, they believe they haven't got enough faith to deal with it.

This reminds me of a story in the Gospel of Luke. The Twelve came to Jesus and said, "Increase our faith" (verse 5 RSV). Jesus told them that if they have faith even the size of a tiny mustard seed, that was enough to uproot a mulberry tree and throw it into the sea (Luke 17:5-6). The tree that Jesus referred to is the black mulberry or sycamine tree (*morus nigra*), which has especially wide and deep roots. Not an easy tree to uproot! But even a little faith is enough to do it.

If even a little faith is enough to do miracles, we should use the faith that we have, even if it isn't much. Faith grows only as we use it. So if we want more faith, the first step is to use the faith that we have. You may have heard it said that faith is like a muscle; it grows only with use.

There's another reason why a little faith is enough. It's not a matter of how much faith we have, it's a matter of whom we put our faith in. We may have only a little faith, but we have a big God. It's his power, not our faith, which works miracles. Our part is to put as much as faith in him as we can and leave the rest to him.

A little faith is enough to work wonders, so let's use the faith that we have. We may have only a little faith, but we have a big God.

ALTHOUGH THE PUBLISHER, the author and Crossroads Christian Communications Inc. have made every effort to ensure that the information in this book was correct at press time, and while this publication is designed to provide accurate information in regard to the subject matter covered, the publisher and the author assume no responsibility for errors, inaccuracies, omissions, or any other inconsistencies herein and hereby disclaim any liability to any party for any loss, damage, or disruption caused by errors or omissions, whether such errors or omissions result from negligence, accident, or any other cause. This publication is meant as a source of inspiration for the reader; however, it is not meant as a substitute for direct expert assistance. If such level of assistance is required, the services of a competent professional should be sought. The content has been provided by the multiple conversations held with the author and Crossroads Christian Communications Inc. and prayer callers. All names and locations have been changed to protect the privacy of all concerned parties.

Bibliography

Adams, Douglas. *The Ultimate Hitchhiker's Guide to the Galaxy*. London: Pan, 2020.
Aland, Kurt et al., eds. *The Greek New Testament* (3rd ed., corrected). Stuttgart: United Bible Societies, 1983.
Attridge, Harold W. and Society of Biblical Literature, eds. *The HarperCollins Study Bible: Fully Revised & Updated*. San Francisco: HarperCollins, 2006.
Bauer, Walter, William F. Arndt, F. Wilbur Gingrich, and Frederick W. Danker. *A Greek-English Lexicon of the New Testament and Other Early Christian Literature*, 2nd edition. Chicago: University of Chicago Press, 1957, 1979.
Boice, James Montgomery. *Philippians: An Expositional Commentary*. Grand Rapids: Zondervan, 1971.
Carter, Matt dir. *Father Brown*, "The Maddest of All," 2014.
———. *Father Brown*, "The Standing Stones," 2015.
Chaffey, Don dir. *The Prisoner*, "Arrival" 1967.
Chesterton, G.K. "The Purple Wig." In *The Complete Father Brown Stories*, 256–267. London: Penguin, 2012.
Doyle, Sir Arthur Conan. *The Penguin Complete Sherlock Holmes, with a Preface by Christopher Morley*. London: Penguin, 1981.
Hoarder-Payton, Gwyneth dir. *NUMB3RS*, "Guilt Trip," 2009.
Hudson, Hugh dir. *Chariots of Fire*, 1981
Hurran, Nick dir. *Sherlock*, "The Lying Detective," 2017.
Jipp, Joshua W. "Hymns in the New Testament," https://www.bibleodyssey.org/en/passages/related-articles/hymns-in-the-new-testament
Kaiser, Walter C. Jr and Duane Garrett eds. *The NIV Archaeological Study Bible: an Illustrated Walk Through Biblical History and Culture*. Grand Rapids: Zondervan, 2005.
King, Hobart M. "How Do Diamonds Form?" https://geology.com/articles/diamonds-from-coal/
Leader, Tony dir., *Star Trek*, "For the World is Hollow and I have Touched the Sky," 1968
Lewis, C.S. *The Chronicles of Narnia*. New York: HarperCollins, 1998.
Liddel, H.G. and and Robert Scott, ed. H.S. Jones. *An Intermediate Greek-English Lexicon*, Oxford: Clarendon, 1980.
Marsh, James dir. *The Theory of Everything*, 2014.
Maloney, David dir. *Doctor Who*, "The Deadly Assassin," 1976.
May, Herbert G. and Bruce M. Metzger eds. *The New Oxford Annotated Bible with the Apocrypha*, expanded ed. New York: Oxford University Press, 1962, 1973.
Meyer, Nicholas dir. *Star Trek II: The Wrath of Khan*. 1982.
Morgan, Andrew dir. *Doctor Who*, "Remembrance of the Daleks." 1988.
Raimi, Sam dir. *Spider-Man* 2002.
Sansom, C.J. *Revelation*. Toronto: Vintage, 2009.
Scott, Ridley dir. *Gladiator*, 2000.
Senensky, Ralph dir. *Star Trek*, "Bread and Circuses," 1967.

Bibliography

Serf, Josef dir. *The Prisoner*, "Many Happy Returns." 1967.
Smax, Willy dir. *Billy Connolly's World Tour of Scotland*, "Episode Six: Edinburgh," 1994.
Spielberg, Steven dir. *Indiana Jones and the Last Crusade*, 1989.
Stevenson, Robert Louis, ed. Robert Mighall. *The Strange Case of Dr. Jekyll and Mr. Hyde and Other Tales of Terror*. London: Penguin, 2003.
Talalay, Rachel dir. *Sherlock*, "The Six Thatchers," 2017.
Taylor, Jud dir. *Star Trek*, "Let That Be Your Last Battlefield," 1969.
Tolkien, J.R.R. *The Lord of the Rings*, 50th anniversary edition. London: HarperCollins, 2005.
Wyler, William dir. *Ben-Hur*, 1959.

www.ingramcontent.com/pod-product-compliance
Lightning Source LLC
Chambersburg PA
CBHW070458100426
42743CB00010B/1677